Super Cheap
The Maldives
Travel Guide 2021

Our Mission

Like Simon Sinek said, "People don't buy what you do; they buy why you do it". We believe strongly that travel can and is best enjoyed on a budget.

Taking a trip to The Maldives is not just an outer journey, it's an inner one. Budget travel brings us closer to locals, culture and authenticity; which in turn makes our inner journeys more peaceful.

Travelling is painted as an expensive hobby; Travel guides, Travel bloggers and influencers often show you overpriced accommodation, restaurants and big-ticket attractions because they make money from our 'we're on vacation' mentality which leads to reckless spending. Our mission is to teach you how to enjoy more for less and get the best value from every rufiyaa you spend in The Maldives.

This guide focuses on the cheap or free in The Maldives, but there is little value in travelling to The Maldives and not experiencing all it has to offer. Where possible we've included cheap workarounds or listed the experience in the loved but costly section - if it is worth your time and money.

We work to dispel myths, save you tons of money, teach you the local tips and tricks and help you find experiences in The Maldives that will flash before your eyes when you come to take your last breath on this beautiful earth.

Who this book is for and why anyone can enjoy budget travel

I've been travelling full-time for 20 years. I don't have a job and I'm not in any debt, which prompts friends and family to ask 'How can you afford to travel?'. My response? 'My passion is finding travel bargains'. This doesn't mean I do any less or sleep in dirty hostels. Someone who spends A LOT on travel hasn't planned or wants to spend their money. I believe you can live the bougie life on a budget; that's what I've been doing for the past 20 years.

Together with thrifty locals I met along the way I have funnelled my passion for travel bargains into 300 travel guides. In this guide, we have formulated a system to pass on to you, so you too can juice everything from visiting The Maldives while spending the least possible money.

There is a big difference between being cheap and frugal. I like to spend money on beautiful experiences, but 20 years of travel has taught me I could have a 20 cent experience that will stir my soul more than a $100 one. Of course, there are times when the reverse is true, my point is, spending money on travel is the best investment you can make but it doesn't have to be at levels set by hotels and attractions with massive ad spends and influencers who are paid small fortunes to get you to buy into something that you could have for a fraction of the cost.

I love travelling because it forces me to be present-minded. I like to have the cold hard budget busting facts to hand (which is why we've included so many one page charts, which you can use as a quick reference), but otherwise, I want to shape my own experience - and I'm sure you do too.

We have designed these travel guides to give you a unique planning tool to experience an unforgettable trip without spending the ascribed tourist budget.

When it comes to FUN budget travel, it's all about what you know. You can have all the feels without most of the bills. A few days spent planning can save you thousands. Luckily, Super Cheap Insider Guides have done the planning for you, so you can distill the information in minutes not days, leaving you to focus on what matters: immersing yourself in the sights, sounds and smells of The Maldives, meeting awesome new people and most importantly, feeling relaxed and happy. My sincere hope is that our tips will bring you great joy at a fraction of the price you expected.

So, grab a cup of tea, put your feet up and relax; you're about to enter the world of enjoying The Maldives on the cheap. Oh and don't forget a biscuit. You need energy to plan a trip of a lifetime on a budget.

Super Cheap The Maldives is <u>not</u> for travellers with the following needs:

1. You require a book with detailed offline travel maps. Super Cheap Insider Guides are best used with Google Maps - download and star our recommendations before you travel to make the most of your time and money.
2. You would like thousands of accommodation, food and attraction recommendations; by definition, cheapest is most often singular. We only include maximum value recommendations. We purposively leave out over-priced attractions when there is no workaround.
3. You would like detailed write-ups about hotels/Airbnbs/Restaurants. We are bargain hunters first and foremost. We dedicate our time to finding the best deals, not writing flowery language about their interiors. Plus things change. If I had a pound for every time I'd read a Lonely Planet description only to find the place completely different, I would be a rich man. Always look at online reviews for the latest up to date information.

If you want to save A LOT of money while comfortably enjoying an unforgettable trip to The Maldives, minus the marketing, hype, scams and tourist traps read on.

Redefining Super Cheap

The value you get out of Super Cheap Maldives is not based on what you paid for it; its based on what you do with it. You can only do great things with it, if you believe saving money is worth your time. Charging things to your credit card and thinking 'oh I'll pay it off when I get back' is something you won't be tempted to do if you change your beliefs now. Think about what you associate with the word cheap, because you make your beliefs and your beliefs make you.

I grew up thinking you had to spend more than you could afford to have a good time travelling. Now I've visited 190 countries I know nothing is further from the truth. Before you embark upon reading our specific tips for The Maldives think about your associations with the word cheap.

Here are the dictionary definitions of cheap:

1. costing very little; relatively low in price; inexpensive:
a cheap dress.
2. costing little labor or trouble:
Words are cheap.
3. charging low prices:
a very cheap store.
4. **of little account; of small value; mean; shoddy:**
cheap conduct; cheap workmanship.
5. **embarrassed; sheepish:**
He felt cheap about his mistake.
6. **stingy; miserly:**
He's too cheap to buy his own brother a cup of coffee.

Three out of six definitions have extremely negative connotations. The 'super cheap' we're talking about in this book is not shoddy, embarrassed or stingy. Hey, you've already donated to charity just by buying this book - how is that stingy? We added the super to reinforce our message. Super's dictionary definition stands for 'a super quality'. Super Cheap stands for enjoying the best on the lowest budget. Question other peoples definitions of cheap so you're not blinded to possibilities, potential, and prosperity. Here are some new associations to consider forging:

Shoddy

Cheap stuff doesn't last is an adage marketing companies have drilled into consumers. However by asking vendors the right questions cheap doesn't mean something won't last, I had a $10 backpack last for 8 years and a $100 suitcase bust on the first journey. A study out of San Francisco University found that people who spent money on experiences rather than things were happier. Memories last forever, not things, even expensive things. And as we will show you during this guide you don't need to pay to create great memories.

Embarrassed

I have friends who routinely pay more to vendors because they think their money is putting food on this person's table. Paradoxically, Cuban doctors are driving taxi's because they earn more money; it's not always a good thing for the place you're visiting to pay more and can cause unwanted distortion in their culture - Airbnb pushing out renters is an obvious example. Think carefully about whether the extra money is helping people or incentivising greed.

Stingy

Cheap can be eco-friendly. Buying thrift clothes is cheap but you also help the Earth. Many travellers are often disillusioned by the reality of traveling experience since the places on our bucket-lists are overcrowded. Cheap can take you away from the crowds. You can find balance and harmony being cheap. Remember,"A journey is best measured in friends, rather than miles." – Tim Cahill. And making friends is free!

A recent survey by Credit Karma found 50% of Millennials and Gen Z get into debt travelling. **Please don't allow credit card debt to be an unwanted souvenir you take home.** As you will see from this book, there's so much you can enjoy in The Maldives for free and so many ways to save money! You just need to want to!

Discover The Maldives

White sand beaches, sparkling blue waters and postcard perfect views, The Maldives is the ultimate tropical paradise. Thanks to its incredible underwater world, rest and relaxation opportunities and the sheer beauty and tranquillity of the islands over a million people visit this tiny, remote Indian Ocean island every year.

The Maldives are made up of 1190 Coral Islands and 26 Atolls. Just 187 of the 1190 islands are inhabited including 106 stand-alone luxury resorts. Though it is constantly billed as a honeymoon and couples destination and it is, the Maldives has much to offer other travellers. The topaz waters surrounding the islands put everything in perspective. Its the type of trip to clean the cobwebs from your soul, but it doesn't have to empty the cash from your wallet.

History

Aryan settlers arrived in The Maldives around 500 BCE. Before
the Islamic period Persian and Arab travellers told that the Maldives was ruled by women. According to legend an Exiled Prince,
Koimala, a nobleman of the Lion Race from Sri Lanka formed
The Maldives because of its strategic importance as a major marine route. Close by Sri Lanka and India have enmeshed their
culture into The Maldives, as the food will reveal. In the 19th cen-
tury The Maldives became a British Protectorate but later
achieved independence in 1965.

In the early 1980s, the Maldives was one of the world's 20 poor-
est countries, with a population of 156,000. In 2012, the population has doubled and life standard have risen thanks to tourism.
The islands have only been a holiday destination for 40 years.

Like any tropical island that caters to tourists, Maldives can be a
budget-buster, but take heart. The trick to keeping your trip cheap
is to get off the tourist track and find the local deals. With a little
planning you can comfortably enjoy Maldives for less than $30 a
day.

INSIDER CULTURAL INSIGHT

The Maldives hold two Guinness World Records. One for being
lowest country in the world (you'll find a maximum elevation
above sea level of 2.4 metres) and one for being the flattest
country in the world.

Planning your trip

When to visit?

The first step in saving money on your Maldives trip is timing. Thankfully The Maldives are hot and sunny all year round. Avoid peak season (December and March) when hotel rooms and flights will triple. You will find cheaper flights and discounted hotel rooms in November and April. Avoid October and June as this is the monsoon season.

The Maldivian are a deeply religious bunch so avoid Islamic holidays especially Eid-Ul-Adha (30 July to 3rd August) as prices for flights and accommodation will skyrocket as returning family members come to celebrate with their families.

The Working Week

Its worth noting the Maldivian working week is Sunday to Thursday; Friday and Saturday are the weekend. On Fridays most businesses are closed. Most shops close for between 15 and 30 minutes at prayer time.

Which island?

Tourists can choose from 100 different islands but in reality that figure is closer to 30. As only 30 have well-developed infrastructure, including ferry terminals, guesthouses, cafes and restaurants, bikini beaches, and diving centres.

The islands are similar to one another topographically and culturally but as an independent traveller the islands you choose make a big difference.

Most people head to popular islands like Maafushi, Thulusdhoo or Rasdhoo as they're close to Male and easy to reach by speed-boat. But for a local experience it's far better to choose islands with less tourists.

We recommend that you choose no more than 3 islands that cater to your needs and desires, otherwise the transfer fees can add up and you'll lose time travelling on ferries.

Sleep cheap and still Luxuriate

If you're dreaming of high-end instagramable over the water water-bungalows resorts you can experience them on a budget. Instead of paying the $600+ a night fees. You can stay in a guesthouse and visit the resorts (if you want) with a day-pass. They start at $50. So you'll pay just one tenth of the overnight fee and get all the perks.

The best budget accommodation

The 400 guesthouses scattered around Maldives are your best option. Staying at a guesthouse island means you can really explore all that the Maldives has to offer in a local way, and you're giving directly back to the community.

Hospitality is extremely important in Islam, so you'll find your hosts to be genuinely caring and obliging. The most delicious Maldivian food is served in family homes so you'll get to try some real Maldivian cuisine.

Plus you can book excursions like snorkelling, diving, surfing and fishing trips through your guesthouse. These excursions are usually half the price of the very same excursions sold at luxury resorts.

You can expect a double en-suite room to cost you about $25 - 50 USD a night including breakfast.

 INSIDER MONEY SAVING TIP

Use Airbnb to book your guesthouse. Airbnb is 25% cheaper than Booking.com or Agoda.

Top 12 guesthouse is-lands

1. Thoddoo – 67 kilometers from Malé, Thoddoo is not far by ferry. There are some incredibly beautiful bikini beaches. Thoddoo is where they grow food for the other islands so its great if you'd like to explore some farms.

2. Dhigurah – almost 100 kilometers from Male, Dhigurah is part of the Alif Dhaal Atoll with a population of jus 500. The main advantage is its home to whale sharks all year round.

3. Thulusdhoo – just north of Malé, you can get here easily by ferry. It is one of the best surfing islands in the Maldives.

4. Maafushi – has the most guesthouses of all the Islands. The first guesthouse in the Maldives opened here in 2010, and it's now the epicentre of tourist visits. Souvenir are cheap in Maafushi. You have a lot of options to dine at all you can eat Buffett restaurant ranging from 10 to 15 USD. Maafushi offers tons of grilled seafood; Grill lobster with rice and shrimp for just 15USD. Alaka guesthouse is great place to stay if you choose to visit Maafushi. Maafushi is a local island with no resorts, but you can visit a lot of different islands from there and there are a ton of water sports for less than you would get at a resort.

5. K.Gulhi island - much less touristy than Maafushi. It has much nicer beaches and it's a shorter ferry ride. Silvershade Guesthouse in K.Gulhi makes for a perfect and cheap stay.

6. Guraidhoo – the perfect combination of an authentic experience plus a nice holiday. Its close to Malé, you can get there by local ferry, and it has a separate bikini island.

7. Rasdhoo - is a tiny island but easy to get to from Malé via ferry. It boasts great diving spots. Rasdhoo Dive Centre is very safe and professional, if you're a first time or hesitant diver definitely

start here. Be mindful that on Rasdhoo island the bikini beach is nice, but very shallow and no swimming is possible.

8. Himmafushi - full of locals who rely on fishing and tourism as their livelihood. They are genuinely friendly. The Jail Break Surf Inn is a luxurious 4-star hotel located in Himmafushi, with consistent last-minute rooms from $30 a night.

9. Ukulhas - offers an incredible natural landscape and some of the best Maldives beaches.

10. Hulhumal - is an artificial island that is suited for a longer vacation. The island is home to a huge array of dining options. The beaches of Hulhumale are beautiful and the lagoon water is turquoise, it's a long enough for a 1 hour walk and is relatively tourist free.

11. Biyadhoo is known as a budget island, the island itself is stunning. Accommodations are basic but the island is pristinely clean. The water is extremely clear and the sand is like sugar. There's excellent snorkelling from the beach and it is known as a resort where divers stay. Getting there is convenient by ferry.

12. Huraa island has a beautiful bikini beach where you can swim and snorkel. The island is not very touristy, so there are limited options for restaurants. Wake&bake has amazing ice-cream and snacks and is very cheap. You can stay at a guesthouse for $50 per night including breakfast for two people (not included 22% tax and service charge). There you can book snorkelling trips to see sharks and turtles for just $20 per person.

The cheapest islands for accommodation (less popular but still offer great beaches and sunbathing) are:

• Embudu
• Meedhupparu
• Meeru
• Chaaya Island
• Dhonveli Vilu Reef
• Ellaidhoo Fihalhoi

Meeru and Dhonveli offer <u>no snorkelling opportunities.</u>

Overly crowded Tourist islands will take a wrecking ball to your bank balance. They are popular for a reason you might say, but there are many incredible things to see, people to meet and food to try on the smaller islands. You'll also be able to negotiate better deals on tours in places with less demand.

If you're planning on staying in guesthouses, be sure to check for five things:

- Whether you book guesthouses on Airbnb or Booking make sure you look for a track record of good reviews.
- A good location relative to the ferry drop off point.
- A lot of guesthouses in the Maldives are called 'Ocean View,' 'Ocean Front' or 'Seaside,' - check the location on Google Maps before booking, many are not near the ocean.
- Make sure you're aware that the smaller islands will be more religious. Maldives is a Muslim country and there are rules you need to abide by, like only wearing a bikini on designated 'bikini beaches'. You can't drink alcohol because of the hosts religion. You can't walk around in your bikini, but its fine at the bikini beaches or in your room.

- You should always confirm which days your guest-house operates pick-ups to not end up stuck at the airport losing a day from your trip.

INSIDER MONEY SAVING TIP

Most guesthouses will tell you there is free wifi, but WiFi is extremely slow on local islands so buy a Maldives sim card at the airport to enjoy 2g and 4G internet on Fulidhoo..

How to ensure your travel insurance covers you for COVID-19

Many insurers stopped selling travel insurance after the start of the pandemic, some have returned with some form of 'COVID-19 cover'. MoneySupermarket.com is updating a list of insurers who cover you for varying degrees of pandemic-related travel disruption. Check on their website before buying a policy to avoid having to wade through the fine print - much of which is not written in plain English and may contain degrees of pandemic coverage such as they will pay your medical expenses but not your flight home. Book hotels and flights with a credit card that cover pandemic-related travel expenses for an added level of security.

REMEMBER if you travel to a country your government is currently advising against travel to for your planned dates, then it's likely that you won't be covered at all.

Hack your The Maldives Accommodation

Your two biggest expenses when travelling to The Maldives are accommodation and food. This section is intended to help you cut these costs dramatically before and while you are in The Maldives.

Hostels are the cheapest accommodation in The Maldives but there are some creative workarounds to upgrade your stay on the cheap.

Use Time

There are two ways to use time. One is to book in advance. Three months will net you the best deal, especially if your visit coincides with an event. The other is to book on the day of your stay. This is a risky move, but if executed well, you can lay your head in a five-star hotel for a 2-star fee.

Before you travel to Maldives, check for big events using a simple google search 'What's on in Maldives', if you find no big events drawing travellers, risk showing up with no accommodation booked (If there are big events on, demand exceeds supply and you should avoid using this strategy). Start checking for discount rooms at 11 am using a private browser on booking.com.

Before I go into demand-based pricing, take a moment to think about your risk tolerance. By risk, I am not talking about personal safety. No amount of financial savings is worth risking that. What I am talking about is being inconvenienced. Do you deal well with last-minute changes?

Can you roll with the punches or do you freak out if something changes? Everyone is different and knowing yourself is the best way to plan a great trip. If you are someone that likes to have everything pre-planned using demand-based pricing to get cheap accommodation will not work for you. Skip this section and go to blind-booking.

Demand-based pricing

Be they an Airbnb host or hotel manager; no one wants empty rooms. Most will do anything to make some revenue because they still have the same costs to cover whether the room is occupied or not. That's why you will find many hotels drastically slashing room rates for same-day bookings.

How to book five-star hotels for a two-star price

You will not be able to find these discounts when the demand exceeds the supply. So if you're visiting during the peak season, or during an event which has drawn many travellers again don't try this.

On the day of your stay, visit booking.com (which offers better discounts than Kayak and agoda.com). Hotel Tonight individually checks for any last-minute bookings, but they take a big chunk of the action, so the better deals come from booking.com. The best results come from booking between 2 pm and 4 pm when the risk of losing any revenue with no occupancy is most pronounced, so algorithms supporting hotels slash prices. This is when you can find rates that are not within the "lowest publicly visible" rate. To avoid losing customers to other websites, or cheapening the image of their hotel most will only offer the super cheap rates during a two hour window from 2 pm to

4 pm. Two guests will pay 10x difference in price but it's absolutely vital to the hotel that neither knows it.

Takeaway: To get the lowest price book on the day of stay between 2 pm and 4 pm and extend your search radius to include further afield hotels with good transport connections.

How to trick travel Algorithms to get the lowest hotel price

Do not believe anyone who says changing your IP address to get cheaper hotels or flights does NOT work. If you don't believe us, download a Tor Network and search for flights and hotels to one destination using your current IP and then the tor network (a tor browser hides your IP address from algorithms. It is commonly used by hackers because websites can't track or predict behaviours). You will receive different prices.

The price you see is a decision made by an algorithm that adjusts prices using data points such as past bookings, remaining capacity, average demand and the probability of selling the room or flight later at a higher price. If booking.-com knows you've searched for the area before it will keep the prices high. To circumvent this, you can either use a different IP address from a cafe or airport or data from an international sim. I use a sim from Three, which provides free data in many countries around the world. When you search from a new IP address, most of the time, and particularly near booking you will get a lower price. Sometimes if your sim comes from a 'rich' country, say the UK or USA, you will see higher rates as the algorithm has learnt people from these countries pay more. The solution is to book from a local wifi connection - but a different one from the one you originally searched from.

How to get last-minute discounts on owner rented properties

In addition to Airbnb, you can also find owner rented rooms and apartments on www.vrbo.com or HomeAway or a host of others. Nearly all owners renting accommodation will happily give renters a "last-minute" discount to avoid the space sitting empty, not earning a dime.

Go to Airbnb or another platform and put in today's date. Once you've found something you like start the negotiating by asking for a 25% reduction. A sample message to an Airbnb host might read:

Dear HOST NAME,

I love your apartment. It looks perfect for me. Unfortunately, I'm on a very tight budget. I hope you won't be offended, but I wanted to ask if you would be amenable to offering me a 25% discount for tonight, tomorrow and the following day? I see that you aren't booked. I can assure you, I will leave your place exactly the way I found it. I will put bed linen in the washer and ensure everything is clean for the next guest. I would be delighted to bring you a bottle of wine to thank you for any discount that you could offer.

If this sounds okay, please send me a custom offer, and I will book immediately.

YOUR NAME.

A polite, genuine message like this, that proposes reciprocity will be successful 80% of the time. Don't ask for more than 25% off, this person still has to pay the bills and will probably say no as your stay will cost them more in bills than they make. Plus starting higher, can offend the owner. Do you want to stay somewhere, where you have offended the host?

In Practice

To use either of these methods, you must travel light. Less stuff means greater mobility, everything is faster and you don't have to check-in or store luggage. If you have a lot of luggage, you're going to have fewer opportunities to save on accommodation. Plus travelling light benefits the planet - you're buying, consuming, and transporting less.

Blind-booking

If your risk tolerance does not allow for last-minute booking, you can use blind-booking. Many hotels in The Maldives not wanting to cheapen their brand with known low-prices, choose to operate a blind booking policy. This is where you book without knowing the name of the hotel you're going to stay in until you've made the payment. This is also sometimes used as a marketing strategy where the hotel is seeking to recover from past issues (commonly bad reviews from poor service). As long as you choose 4 or 5 star hotels, you will find them to be clean, comfortable and safe. priceline.com, Hot Rate® Hotels and Top Secret Hotels (operated by lastminute.com) offer the best deals in The Maldives.

Hotels.com Loyalty Program

This is currently the best hotel loyalty program with hotels in The Maldives. The basic premise is you collect 10 nights and get 1 free. hotels.com price match, so if booking.com has a cheaper price you can get hotel.com, to match. If you intend to travel more than ten nights in a year, its a great choice to get the 11th free.

Don't let time use you.

Rigidity will cost you money. You pay the price you're willing to pay, not the amount it requires a hotel to deliver. Therefore if you're in town for a big event, saving money on accommodation is nearly impossible so in such cases book three months ahead.

Use our FREE accommodation finder service

Feeling overwhelmed by all the accommodation options in The Maldives? Save yourself the stress, hassle and time by using our FREE accommodation finder service.

We pride ourselves on actively helping our readers find the best price-performance accommodation. We normally charge $50 for this service, but for our paid readers it is FREE when you leave an honest review of this book. (Just a few short words like 'Good budget tips and insider insights' is all it takes).

So, how do you use the service?

Simply send our Services Manager, Amy Abraham the following information:

1. A screenshot proof of purchase. (Go to your Amazon account, and click orders and make a screenshot of your purchase.)
2. Send a screenshot of your review of the guide on Amazon.
3. Send answers to the following questions:

- What's your Budget? (e.g. lowest possible)
- How many are travelling and what are their ages? (e.g. do you need a baby bed?)
- What Approximate location do you desire? (e.g. as close to the centre as possible/ near public transport)
- Do you have a strong dislike of either hostels or Airbnbs?

- If anyone in your group has mobility restrictions/ requires a lift/ no stairs etc?
- Add any details you think are pertinent to your needs.

About Amy and her team

Amy has travelled to over 170 countries personally and has recruited a team of bargain hunters to provide our accommodation finder service.

Send your details via E-mail to Amy Abraham at Amy@supercheapinsiderguides.com

Make a request via Facebook

We also accept accommodation search requests via Facebook messenger, just make sure you send the necessary information listed above. You can find us here: https://www.facebook.com/SuperCheapInsiderGuides/

What you'll receive

Amy and her team will work their magic. Within 24 hours you will be sent a list of the top three accommodations for your specific needs prioritised by which one we recommend.

(Please note: If you received this book for free as part of a promotion, we cannot extend this service to you.)

We offer the same service for finding you the cheapest most direct flight. See our cheapest route to The Maldives for details.

Saving money on Maldives Food

Breakfast

If you stay somewhere with a free breakfast, eat smart. Don't eat sugary cereals or white flour rich pastries if you don't want to be hungry an hour later. Before leaving your hotel or checking out, find some fresh fruit, water, and granola in the fitness centre or coffee in the lobby or business centre. If your hotel doesn't have free breakfast, don't take it. You can always eat cheaper outside. Belle Amie Bistro Malé, Maldives has the best cheap breakfast we found. Here you can pick up breakfast for less than $3.

Visit supermarkets at discount times

You can get a 50 per cent discount around 5 pm at the Red Wave supermarkets on fresh produce.

Eat Street food

You can eat for under three dollars from street vendors. Some worry about eating street food, but as long as you follow where the locals are queuing you'll never have any problems.

Alcohol is Available Only in Resorts and Hotels.

It's illegal to bring alcohol with you in your bags. Indulge in happy hours at resort bars to save money on drinks (5pm - 7pm)

How to be a green tourist in Maldives

Due to climatic changes including rising sea levels and increasing land erosion, the islands of The Maldives are being adversely affected. Coral levels are plummeting and the government has strict laws in place to prevent further damage and degradation since the severe bleaching that occurred in 2016. 80% of the country's land is coral islands less than one metre above sea level, so The Maldives sinking is a very real possibility, so it's important as responsible tourists that we help not hinder The Maldives. There is a bizarre misconception that you have to spend money to travel in an eco-friendly way. This like, all marketing myths was concocted and hyped by companies seeking to make money. Anything with eco in front of their names e.g Eco-tours will be triple the cost of the regular tour. Don't get me wrong, sometimes its best to take these tours if you're visiting endangered areas. However, in most instances such places have extensive legislation that everyone, including the eco and non-eco tour companies must comply with. The vast majority of ways you can travel eco-friendly are free and even save you money:

- Avoid Bottled Water - get a good water bottle and refill. The water in The Maldives is not safe to drink. Tap water in Maldives is all treated rainwater and it's not advisable to drink it. Stay somewhere with a kettle or stove. You can then boil water, cool and refill safely.
- Don't put it in a plastic bag, bring a cotton tote with you when you venture out.
- Pack Light - this is one of the best ways to save money. If you find a 5-star hotel for tonight for $10, and you're at an Airbnb or hostel, you can easily pack and upgrade hassle-free. A light pack equals freedom and it means less to wash.
- Travel around The Maldives on Bikes or use Public Transportation.

- Walk, this is the best way to get to know The Maldives. You never know what's around the corner especially in Malé!
- Travel Overland - this isn't always viable especially if you only have limited time off work, but where possible avoid flying and if you have to compensate by off-setting or keeping the rest of your trip carbon-neutral by doing all of the above.

Before we begin here is a snapshot of how you can enjoy a $3,000 trip to Maldives for $300

A fully costed breakdown will be explained at the end of this guide.

Stay	You can find an Airbnb in Maldives from $30 a night Here is the link to a perfect Airbnb: https://www.airbnb.com/rooms/9969407?s=51 $49 entire apartment for four people. Stay in Guesthouses for $25/night. Or there's the option to use our free accommodation finder service.
Eat	Average meal cost: $3 – $6. Teashops are super cheap, but women should take a companion with them; they are heavily dominated by local men.
Move	Public ferries and bike.
See	Snorkel, dive and lounge on The Beaches or in 5-star hotels during the day, explore Mosques, museums, markets and watch the remarkable sunsets.

Total	US$300

Unique bargains I love in The Maldives

The Maldives has the reputation of being among the most luxurious and expensive destinations in the world. Fortunately, some of the best things in life are free. Exploring the islands, atolls and beaches is cheap by ferry. The markets and teashops are a great place to grab a cheap lunch and souvenirs.

A stay in a guesthouse will cost you a fraction of the price of a luxury Maldives resorts. Depending on the island, it's also possible that you find some bargain tours bookable from your guesthouse. Dolphin sunset cruise cost as little as $30 in the low-season. You may find yourself to be one of just a handful of tourists staying on the smaller islands, and when demand is low, you can get the best prices.

The Maldives offers a wealth of opportunities to experience the islands for free, from strolls through Malé soaking up the culture, to a number of cheap museums, exhibitions, public buildings and mosques, as well as fabulous free entertainment and amazing day resort passes to hotels charging $1,000 a night.

Even the most reluctant bargain hunter can be successful in The Maldives. Once you uncover so many bargains you'll be thinking about booking your next trip to this tropical paradise.

 ## INSIDER MONEY SAVING TIP

In Male, public toilets charge Rf2. Use toilets in cafes and restaurants in Male – they're cleaner and free.

How to use this book

Google and Tripadvisor are your on-the-go guides while travelling, a travel guide adds the most value during the planning phase, and if you're without wifi. Always download the google map for your destination - having an offline map will make using Super Cheap The Maldives much more comfortable. For ease of use, we've set the book out the way you travel starting with arriving, how to get around, then on to the money-saving tips. The tips we ordered according to when you need to know the tip to save money, so free tours and combination tickets feature first. We prioritised the rest of the tips by how much money you can save and by how likely it was that you would be able to find the tip with a google search. Meaning those we think you could find alone are nearer the bottom. I hope you find this layout useful. If you have any ideas about making Super Cheap Insider Guides easy to use, please email me philgtang@gmail.com

A quick note on how we Source Super Cheap Tips

We focus entirely on finding the best bargains. We give each of our collaborators $2,000 to hunt down never-before-seen deals. The type you either only know if you're local or by on the ground research. The actual writing and editing are done for free by four people (see who are writers are at the end of the book). As we grow, we will hire more writers to pen fabulous prose, but for now, we are in the nuts and bolts of hunting down unbelievable deals. We do this yearly, which means we just keep finding more amazing ways for you to have the same experience for less, but that's also why if you read or listen more of our guides, you may find the sentence structure familiar. Like many other guide book companies (Lonely Planet, Rough Guides etc) we use a content management system (ie, we repurpose some text). We'd like to be upfront about this so if you read or listen to another of our guides you aren't annoyed. Its worth mentioning that we pride ourselves on being a hands-on travel guide, and we put substantial resource behind helping you find the cheapest flight (explained in a moment) and the best value accommodation.

Another way you can save and make money is to apply to become one of our local collaborators at supercheapinsiderguides.com. We require you to identify a minimum of 250 super cheap tips and you need to live in the area you research. When you hear INSIDER HISTORICAL INSIGHT or INSIDER CULTURAL INSIGHT or INSIDER MONEY SAVING TIP this is a specific tip our insider contributed. Now let's get started with juicing the most pleasure from your trip to Maldives with the least possible money.

WARNINGS: The Taxes and Fees

The Maldivian government charge you a lot of taxes and theres no way to avoid them. Here's the breakdown:

For every night you spend in the Maldives you will pay an $8 bed tax. $8 per person per night.

You pay an 8% GST (sales tax) for the room.

There is a 10% service charge. Guesthouse owners try to get you to pay this fee in US dollars, but if you don't have any they will accept Maldivian Rufiyaa (which will work out cheaper for you).

If you stay at a guesthouse that takes credit cards, don't plan to pay with one they charge you 4% EXTRA to do so.

OUR SUPER CHEAP TIPS

Here are our specific super cheap tips for enjoying a $3,000 trip to Maldives for just $300.

Cheapest route to The Maldives from America

At the time of writing China Eastern are flying to Male for $427 return. Phil's day job for the past 15 years has been

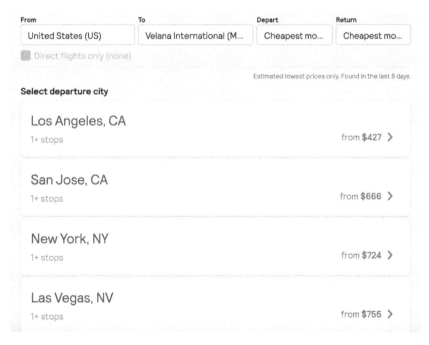

From	To	Depart	Return
United States (US)	Velana International (M...	Cheapest mo...	Cheapest mo...

Direct flights only (none)

Estimated lowest prices only. Found in the last 8 days.

Select departure city

Los Angeles, CA
1+ stops · from **$427** >

San Jose, CA
1+ stops · from **$666** >

New York, NY
1+ stops · from **$724** >

Las Vegas, NV
1+ stops · from **$755** >

finding cheap flights for blue chip companies, so if you need help finding a cheap flight Phil can help you for free. Simply review this book and send him an email. philgtang@gmail.com (Please send a screenshot of your review - with your flight hacking request). Phil aims to reply to you within 12 hours. If it's an urgent request mark the email URGENT in the subject line and he will endeavour to reply ASAP.

Cheapest route to The Maldives from Europe

At the time of writing Condor are flying to Maldives direct from Frankfurt for around $350 return.

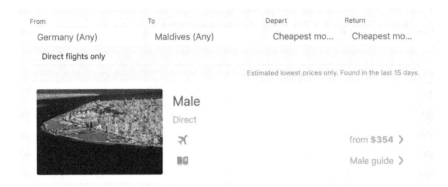

From	To	Depart	Return
Germany (Any)	Maldives (Any)	Cheapest mo...	Cheapest mo...
Direct flights only			

Estimated lowest prices only. Found in the last 15 days.

Male
Direct

✈

from **$354** ⟩

Male guide ⟩

Note: The cheapest flights are from Bangkok and Kuala Lumpur making The Maldives a perfect addition to your SE Asia trip! Expect to pay $180 return from Bangkok.

💡 INSIDER INSIGHT

When flying in or out of Male book a window seat on the left side of the plane, this is where you get to see the beautiful atolls. On AirAsia the seat cost is only $3.

Arriving

Most international flights arrive at Male International Airport. Its the main international airport hub the Maldives. Its on the Hulhule Island in the North Male Atoll, near the capital island Male. The cheapest way from the island to Malé and other islands is with the public ferry. Tickets cost $3.

 INSIDER MONEY SAVING TIP

Don't arrive late at night
Many international planes arrive in the Maldives close to midnight. After a lengthy journey to the Maldives and a late night arrival plan to stay the night on Hulhumale Island (airport island). The ferries don't run after midnight and you can expect to pay from US$200 for a late night 45-minute private speedboat transfer, one way.

 INSIDER INSIGHT

There are four other international airports in Maldives: Velana International Airport, Gan International Airport, Hanimaadhoo International Airport, and Villa International Airport. Flights between the islands are expensive and its always much cheaper to take the ferry.

Getting around

Transport is a cost that can quickly add up but there are ways to save while exploring The Maldives; Island hopping by public ferry is 20 times cheaper than speedboats or domestic flights.

Public ferries

Local ferries depart Male and cost US$2. You can travel about three hours between various islands. Speedboats are great for quicker travel but cost $30 - 50. Each public ferry has set arrival and departure time, and usually only makes one return journey each day. Ferries in the Maldives are reliable (although weather dependent). No Ferries depart on Fridays and Saturdays (the weekend in Maldives) so time your travel right.

Unfortunately, you can't easily Google for ferry times. Your guesthouse or the ferry departure point can advise you on ferry times, just ask. There's no pre-booking and the schedules are reliable if you can find them but they are hard to locate.

Speedboats

The speedboat ride to most islands is under an 1 hour and cost from $30 - $50.

Cycle

The Maldives is a lovely country to cycle because its so flat. A lot of guesthouses have free bikes and others rent cheaply.

Walk – it's the best way to discover. Just bring sun-lotion, a hat and aftersun. Its expensive to buy toiletries in The Maldives.

Book tours only once you arrive

If you are a planner, it's your norm to book tours and excursions in advance wait until you arrive in The Maldives to save a pretty penny on your tours. Don't worry about tours filling up, literally every resort and guesthouse on the local islands offers the same tours so you can join from any. The weather can be unpredictable in the Maldives so even if you book ahead you may find your itinerary changing unexpectedly.

Get Cultured in Malé before you head to other islands

Start your Maldivian adventure by spending a night or two in Malé, the mercantile capital where over a third of the Maldivian population lives. Malé is one of the world's smallest national capitals. Stroll its narrow street and have a look at a mix of shops museums, some interesting markets and ancient mosques.

National Art Gallery
Situated very close to the Sultan Park, this library and art gallery houses temporary displays of Maldivian art in a modern building. Museum entry is $4.

The National Museum

The museum presents a wide array of historic artefacts ranging from the Maldives' Buddhist era through the Islamic monarchs, depicting the rich and historical culture of The Maldives. The Police exhibition shows a history of Maldives Police department shown on video screens. Museum fees is $6 per person and $1 for one device for photography.

 INSIDER TIP

Maldives has its own semi-submerged art gallery, the Coralarium at Fairmont Maldives Sirru Fen Fushi. It's 33 km from Hanimaadhoo International Airport and worth a visit if you're going to that airport.

Mosque Hop in Male

Not only exceptional architecturally and historically, The Mal-

dives's mosques contain exquisite art, artefacts and other priceless treasures. Best of all, entry to general areas within them is, in most cases, free. Visit the Malé Mosque, also known as the

Malé Friday Mosque or the Malé Hukuru Miskiy or Old Friday Mosque. It is an ornate 1658 mosque made of coral stones, features sea-culture architecture.

Unlike other mosques, here you can go inside, always leave shoes at the door and be respectful to locals. Women must be wearing long pants and a scarf to cover shoulders and any exposed skin and hair. Its a good place to blend in with local culture and get to know more about religion in Maldives.

 INSIDER CULTURAL INSIGHT

The Call to Prayer happens four times throughout the day starting at dawn. Men attend prayers at least once a day, while women pray at home.

Visit the markets

Malé markets are a fun and eye-opening plunge into local culture and, unless you succumb to the persistent vendors, it will cost you nothing. At the Fish Market Fishermen lay out daily catches of tuna and other fish on the tiled floor of this open marketplace. It makes for great photo opportunities.
Address: 188 Ibrahim Hassan Didi Magu.

The Chaandanee Magu is another popular street market. Here you'll find grilled fish, typical Maldivian cuisine includes tuna with onion and lime juice, sweet and thick milk tea, and roshi flatbreads – similar to an Indian roti.

 INSIDER INSIGHT

Be careful of mopeds in Malé. They whip around narrow streets at speed.

Experience pure luxury for a 10th of the price

Experience all the luxury during the day and lay your head somewhere cheap at night with resort day passes.

Almost all resorts in The Maldives offer day passes depending upon the timing and resort that you want to visit. They range from $50 to $90 for the day. You'll get access to a private island, bikini beach, a nice lunch, drinks including alcohol,, towels, showers and snorkelling equipment. Here are the best resorts to consider:

1.   LUX South Ari Atoll, Maldives
2.   Hurawalhi Island Resort
3.   Kudadoo Maldives Private Island

4.   Shangri-La's Villingili Resort & Spa, Maldives

You can book directly with the front desk of any hotel, es-pecially on Maafushi. Otherwise, contact the resort by phone or e-mail before you intend to go to make sure they are offering day passes on the day you wish to visit. Many host weddings for thousands of people and will restrict day-passes during such events. Travelling this way will save you $550 a day on the same experience! Plus you can access alcohol and enjoy 2 for 1 happy hour cocktails at the resort beach bars.

Go Scuba diving on the cheap

Thanks to the clear waters and year round high visibility, The Maldives boasts some of the best diving and snorkelling in the world. Take some time to explore the world beneath the water, arguably its the best thing The Maldives has to offer. You'll find manta rays, whale sharks and dolphins, Napoleon wrasse, giant clams, colourful soft coral, turtles and vast legions of eagle ray.

There are two seasons for diving in the Maldives:

1. December to April for encountering manta rays and whale sharks,
2. May to December for other shark species and other marine animals who enjoy slightly colder water.

Here are the best bang for your buck diving sites in The Maldives:

1. Dharavandhoo is home to Manta ray and many whale sharks.

2. Maafushi, an abudance of marine life and lots of eagle rays.

3. Rasdhoo, an abundance of tuna , sharks , turtles, and various rays.

4. Omadhoo in Ari Atoll is 70 kms from Male. About 800 people live on Omadhoo. It is a world famous dive destination.

5. For a free alternative you can swim for free with Manta Rays at Manta Point on Lankanfinolhu.

Always choose a dive centre that gives you a good feeling in terms of safety and reviews. Your host can normally advise on the best ones. Dives typically range from $50 to $150.

Most famous dive sites in The Maldives:
- Alimatha House Reef - up to 100 nurse sharks.
- Miyaru Kandu - translates as 'Shark Channel'.
- Fulidhoo Caves - deep overhangs covered in soft coral. This is the place for great night dives.

Try Wreck Diving
Many ships have sunk in Indian Ocean. The Victory Wreck which sunk in 1981 is the most famous wreck to dive. It just reopened after 3 years of closure. the other options include: Kuda Giri, Halaveli Wreck, Fesdu Wreck, The British Loyalty, The Liffey and the Utheemu 1 and 2 and Khuda Maa. Ask around at your guesthouse, there are many tourist packages for wreck diving. The cost can be as low as 4,000Rs, $52USD.

INSIDER CULTURAL INSIGHT

Book dives ahead of time, confirming the total price and shop around between resorts and guesthouses to find the best deals.

The best islands for snorkelling

Snorkeling is easy to learn and does not require extensive training, like diving and its great for kids and easy for adults. Here are the best places to snorkel in The Maldives:

- The Ari atoll encloses some of the most wonderful islands and beaches of the archipelago.
- Thoddoo offers great Snorkeling, manta ray, and beach
- Lily Beach.
- Filitheyo Island.
- Bandos Island.
- Park Hyatt Maldives Hadahaa (you have to pay for a day pass)
- Ranveli is a pretty little island with a smaller house reef on the north side.
- Athuruga has one of the best reefs.
- A budget island with a very good reef to snorkel is Embudu.

The best beaches

While some beaches may boast softer granules than others, the basic fact remains: all beaches across the atolls have whiter-than-white powder sands and bright-blue waters. Go to almost any and you'll be hypnotised by the rhythmic blue waves. Here are the two beaches that never fail to impress:

1. Reethi Rah - A tiny island with beaches of the type you always dream of when wanting to escape to paradise.
2. Cocoa Island on the South Male Atoll is a 5-star hotel, that you'd need a day pass to visit. But its so worth it. The beach is simply breathtaking.

INSIDER CULTURAL INSIGHT

Nearly all inhabited islands with guesthouses have 'bikini beaches'. Guesthouses on islands without bikini beaches often offer day trips to deserted islands where tourists can strip down without fear of offending the locals.

Look out for The Glow In Dark Beach phenomena

Bioluminescence creates what literally looks like stars in the sea in The Maldives. You can see it anywhere if, and only if the conditions are right; the sea planktons are believed to be responsible for it. Look out for little blue specs on the beach at night. If you drag your feet you'll get streaks of blue. You're more likely to see it on darker beaches. We usually see it around midnight on various beaches around the Maldives away from man-made light.

Go out to Sea on a Dhoni

A dhoni is a traditional Wooden Sailboat. It's the oldest sea vessel in the Maldives. They used to be built using coconut palm timber without any plans! Your guesthouse can help you arrange this and other tours such as visiting sandbanks, dolphin sunset trips. They only cost between $15 - 60 USD depending on the activity, length and demand.

Watch a Bodu Beru Performance

During one of your day-pass visits try to catch a Bodu Beru performance. The word means 'big drum' in Dhivehi. This dance and drum show is performed by all-male performers who seem to enter a trance-like state as the music builds.

Enjoy a massage

Travelling can be stressful. A good massage calms the nervous system and relieves tension. The best bang for your buck massage in The Maldives is undoubtably Duniye Spa in Malé. If you go during happy hour 2pm - 4pm you can get 10USD off a full price massage. https://www.duniyespas.com/

Practical tips

Be sensitive to the locals
Maldivians are conservative Muslims. They are tolerant people, but you should dress modesty to avoid offence. n places such as Maafushi where tourism dominates the rules are more relaxed, but in other areas women should wear long skirts, cover their shoulders and avoid low-cut tops. Men can get away with shorts, but don't walk about bare-chested. Locals tend to be shy but will always help you. Locals will also be more open if you respect the island's dress code.

Public beaches v Bikini beaches
On public beaches it is not allowed to wear a bikini, therefore there are separate bikini beaches. If one isn't within reach, take a dip in a loose t-shirt, as the locals do. The good thing about buying resort passes is that you don't need to worry about offending anyone.

Alcohol
Alcohol is strictly forbidden on local islands in Maldives, but there is a solution for those really craving a drink for sunset. Offshore Fulidhoo there is a boat that holds a license to sell alcohol to foreigners, it is not always around, but you can always give it a call. There is a sign at the bikini beach with a phone number.

Pay in local currency (Maldivain Rufiyaa)
It's much cheaper than paying in US Dollars. Paying in cash makes your money go a little further. Some guesthouse islands do not have ATM's and none will accept cards. So be sure to stock up on the local currency at the airport before departing to your island. Ferries and local shops will only accept rufiyaa.

Plan your ferry trips in advance
If you want to travel by public ferry to keep costs down, you'll have to plan in advance as they don't run every day. atolltransfer-.com

Be very careful what you pack
Don't take any of these items into The Maldives (they are strictly prohibited and you may find yourself arrested):

• Any materials contrary to Islam; Alcohol; Pornographic materials; Pork products; Narcotics

Don't eat in public during Ramadan
During Ramadan, the month of fasting, all cafes will be closed in the day although you can still order food from your guesthouse, it would be rude to eat in front of others who cannot. Though this is an acceptable practice at most resorts.

Not super cheap but loved

Whale Shark Diving

There is no particular time to spot these incredible creatures but luck play a role. According to experts May, November and December are the best time to see them. Sun Island Resort and Spa on the Nalaguraidhoo island of South Ari Atoll is the best place to see them. Make sure you go with a trustworthy company and check reviews to make sure they don't support the snorkelers or divers touching the sharks. This is highly unethical. Dhigurah also has lots of daily sightings. Again, choose your company wisely. Prices start at $180 per person, so its not super cheap, but very loved.

Underwater dining

Indulge in gourmet food at Ithaa Undersea Restaurant. Ithaa, which means mother-of-pearl in Dhivehi, is an undersea restaurant 5 metres below sea level at the Conrad Maldives Rangali Island in Alif Dhaal Atoll. Expect to pay a whopping $238 for two to lunch. Dining will set you back $380.

Don't leave without considering visiting:

Ari Atoll
This large natural atoll consists of 105 islands, with over 20 only tourist resorts. If you want to resort hop, this is the place to do it.

Rasdhoo
Clear waters and diving areas draw travellers to this compact island known for its striking scenery.

Villingili
Small, laid-back resort island with beaches, guest houses, water sports and a golf course.

Mirihi
This petite island is known for its high-end resort, scuba diving and striking tropical setting.

Huraa
This tiny island features a resort, water recreation, eateries & shops in a scenic natural setting.

Meedhupparu
Tiny isle featuring a white-sand beach and contemporary lodging, plus snorkeling in coral reef.

Huvadhu Atoll
Huvadhu is a large atoll located south of the Suvadiva Channel the Republic of Maldives. With a total area of 3152 km², of which 38.5 km² is dry land, it is the second largest geographical atoll. It's under explored because its expensive to get to from Male.

Is the tap water drinkable?

No, boil water to refill your water bottle and cut costs on buying water.

How much can you save haggling here?

Some good-humoured bargaining at smaller artisan or craft shops or guesthouses in the low season is not unusual if you are making multiple purchases or staying for some time, but Maldives is no Bangkok.

Need to Know

Currency: Maldivian Rufiyaa

Language: Dhivehi and English.

Money: Widely available ATMs.

Visas: http://www.doyouneedvisa.com/ Nobody coming to Maldives requires a visa for a stay of 30 days or less.

Time: GMT + 5

Important Numbers

102 Ambulance

119 Police

Watch to understand the History

Maldives 's history is fascinating. There are tons of documentaries. This is great - https://www.youtube.com/watch?v=Yvc_hoenl-U

Food and drink hacks

Eat at teashops

These simple local cafes serve up cheap and delicious hedhikaa ('short eats'). They are extremely cheap and the best place to try local dishes and interact with Maldivians. Go in groups, they are very male dominated and lone women may feel like pariahs.

Short eat savoury eats to try:

- Fihunu mas - fish pieces coated in chilli
- Keemia - fried fish rolls
- Kuli boakiba - spicy fish cakes
- Gulha - dough balls filled with fish and spices.

Sweet eats to try:

- bondi bai (rice pudding),
- fried bananas in dough

Best bang for your buck all-you-can-eat

All you can eat buffets are a great way to stock on on nutritious food while travelling. Dishes like fish are normally expensive, but at Salt Café & Restaurant you can chow down on your omega 3's for much less. A buffet in Malé is typically $10 - $15.

Eat Street Food

You don't have to spend a lot to eat the most incredible food in The Maldives. Traditional Maldivian cuisine is based on three ingredients: coconut, fish, and with grains or vegetables. Go where the locals are queuing for great street eats.

Cheap Eats

it's VERY easy to have an overpriced meal on the Maldives. **Fill your stomach without emptying your wallet by trying these local restaurants with mains under $8 or by eating Maldivian foods at local island teaships to gain both an insight into culture and to help your bank account.**

Fish is the staple diet of Maldives: Tuna Maldives' favourite fish, the core ingredient of many hedhikaa (Maldivian finger snacks) and also eaten dried, stewed, grilled, and for breakfast! Swordfish. Octopus Not often found in resorts, but loved on inhabited islands, and typically served in a curry sauce.

Note: Download the offline map for Maldives on Google maps, (instructions 1. go to app 2. select offline apps in the left sidebar 3. go to the area you want to download 4. click download). Then simply type the restaurant names in to navigate, add the restaurants to your favourites by clicking the star icon so you can see where the cheap eats are when you're out and about to avoid wasting your money at hyped tourist joints)

Salt Café & Restaurant
Delicious All you can eat in Malé with very reasonable prices.

Thoum
Middle Eastern fast food place serving cheap kebabs in Malé.

Seaside Grill Maldives
The grill tastes sensational and the pricing was very good compared to nearby options on Hulhumale.

Citron by Lemongrass
All you can eat. Great for evening tea with short eats as in Malé.

Pizza Mia
Vegetarian pizza options in Malé. Good for kids

Bombay Darbar
Tasty and affordable Indian food on Hulhumale. Cash only.

Belle Amie Bistro
The best for cheap eats in Malé.

Symphony Restaurant
All you can eat family friendly restaurant in Malé.

Contagious Pizza
Great food, very kind staff, family run business, card magic show for kids on Thulusdhoo.

Sala Thai
Cheap romantic Thai dinner in Malé.

Nouvelle Grill & Restaurant
Best grilled food in Malé. Try their chicken tikka rice.

Getting Out of Maldives cheaply

At the time of writing Indigo are offering the cheapest flights onwards. Take advantage of discounts and specials. Sign up for e-newsletters from local carriers including Indigo to learn about special fares. Be careful with cheap airlines, most will allow hand-luggage only, and some charge for anything that is not a backpack. Check their websites before booking if you need to take luggage.

From	To	Depart	Return
Maldives (Any)	Everywhere	Cheapest mo...	(One Way)
Direct flights only			

Estimated lowest prices only. Found in the last 15 days.

Maldives	from $78	⌄
Malaysia	from $95	⌄
Singapore	from $107	⌄
India	from $108	⌄
Thailand	from $113	⌄
Germany	from $115	⌄

Avoid these tourist traps or scams

Alcohol
Bringing alcohol to Maldives is prohibited. Visit an all-inclusive resort to have a drink.

Water
Bottled water is extremely expensive in Maldives and tourists have reported paying upwards of $10 for 1.5 liters of water. Make sure your room has a kettle so you can boil and refill your water or filtered water dispenser.

Souvenirs
Do not buy the sea shells and dried corals available. Most countries prohibit their import and you could face huge fines even, if as locals claim, they are 'certified'. Leave the shells and coral where they should be: in the ocean.

Speed boat transfers
If you take one, agree the price before boarding the boat to avoid being scammed. And pay in the Rufiyaa.

RECAP: How to have a $3,000 trip to The Maldives on a $300 budget

Stay in Guesthouses
Maldivian guesthouses truly provide the best and most authentic experience for the lowest cost. Potential saving $1,800.

Resort passes
Indulge in the high-life during the day and lay your head someone cheap at night. Try out a day pass for unbridled luxury, with 132 resorts located in the different atolls you'll spoilt for choice. Potential saving $2,000.

Restaurant deals
Nearly every local restaurant in The Maldives offers a mid-day menu for lunch at around $10. If you're on a budget, but like eating out, consider doing your dining in the day-time. Potential saving $300.

Do all the free stuff first
The natural environment in The Maldives is an endless bounty of interesting and inspiring things to experience not to mention gawp at. Start free and be mindful of what you want to pay for. Potential savings: $200.

Book your tours in person at your guesthouse
This is how you get the best rates. Potential savings: $500.

Book Ahead

Book six weeks ahead for the lowest prices on outward buses and flights. Potential savings: $300

Fully costed Break-down

	How	Cost normally	Cost when following suggested tip
How I got from the city	Plan to arrive during the day and take the ferry	$100	$3
Where I stayed	Guesthouse booked on Airbnb- share to bring down cost. Airbnb for 7 days housing 4 people - so technically $12.50 a night per person	Luxury resorts are upwards of $500 a night.	$50 a day, shared $12.50 a day.
Tastiest street foods I ate and cost	Seafood.	Follow the locals for massive savings on food.	$5 - $20
How I got around	Ferry and bike	See if you can share speedboats to save cash.	$60
What I saw and paid	Free attractions: beaches, snorkelling, luxury resorts and free live music performances.	Diving is a must-do, but you can do it for under $50 a dive.	$150
My onward flight	Onward flight to Kuala Lumpur		$57

My Total costs	US380		$300	

PRACTICAL THINGS TO REMEMBER TO SAVE MONEY IN THE MALDIVES

- Download google maps for for use offline for each island you plan to visit. It will save you being ripped off by opportunistic cab drivers.
- Download the Dhivehi language pack on google translate - you will be grateful you have it! The camera function is great for translating local menus.
- Bring a good mosquito spray or combine a few drops of lemongrass oil with a moisturiser. This is the technique the Inca's used to keep mosquitos at bay. The smell turns the mosquitos away from your skin. Mosquitoes vary from non-existent to very troublesome depending on which island you're on and what time of year it is. In general, mosquitoes aren't a huge problem because there are few areas of open freshwater where they can breed and most resorts spray their islands to eradicate mosquitoes but budget travellers are definitely more affected by them. Bring the lemongrass oil!
- Know the names of foods to try and star three teashops or restaurants to try them at.
- Don't eat at any restaurants with touts outside. Go away from the main thoroughfares for cheaper restaurant prices.
- Get Rufiyaa at the airport when you land and take enough to pay for everything in cash. Paying on your card or in another currency will only result in you being ripped off.
- Avoid over-scheduling. You don't want to pack so much into your trip you wind up feeling like you're working on the conveyor belt called best sights of Maldives instead of fully saturating your senses in the incredible sights, sounds, smells of the Maldives.

- Pack a travel snorkel kit if you plan to snorkel. Its a great free activity when you have your own equipment.
- Identify resorts you want to experience during the day.
- Pack food for the airport, you'll save $10 on a bad cup of coffee and stale croissant.

Print or screenshot for easy reference

	How	Cost
Get from the airport	Ferry $3	$30
Stay	Airbnb for 7 days housing 4 people - so technically $12.50 a night per person	$87
Food	Average meal cost: $10 - see cheap eats section.	$5 - $10 per meal
Get around	Ferries and cycling	$15 for all rides
See	Free attractions: beaches, snorkelling, luxury resorts and free live music performances.	$150
Get out	Onward flight to Kuala Lumpur	$57
Total	US$300	$300

The secret to saving HUGE amounts of money when travelling to The Maldives is...

Your mindset. Money is an emotional topic, if you associate words like cheapskate with being thrifty when travelling you are likely to say 'F-it' and spend your money needlessly because you associate pain with saving money. You pay now for an immediate reward. Our brains are prehistoric; they focus on surviving day to day. Travel companies and hotels know this and put trillions into making you believe you will be happier when you spend on their products or services. Our poor brains are up against outdated programming and an onslaught of advertisements bombarding us with the message: spending money on travel equals PLEASURE. To correct this carefully lodged propaganda in your frontal cortex you need to imagine your future self.

Saving money does not make you a cheapskate. It makes you smart. How do people get rich? They invest their money. They don't go out and earn it; they let their money earn more money. So every time you want to spend money, imagine this: while you travel your money is working for you, not you for money. While you sleep the money you've invested is going up and up. That's a pleasure a pricey entrance fee can't give you. Thinking about putting your money to work for you tricks your brain into believing you are not withholding pleasure from yourself, you are saving your money to invest so you can go to even more amazing places. You are thus turning thrifty travel into a pleasure fueled sport.

When you've got money invested - If you want to splash your cash on a first-class airplane seat - you can. I can't tell you how to invest your money, only that you should. Saving $20 on taxi's doesn't seem like much but over time you could be saving upwards of $15,000 a year, which is a deposit for a house which you can rent on Airbnb to finance more travel. Your brain making money looks like your brain on cocaine, so tell yourself saving money is making money.

Scientists have proved that imagining your future self is the easiest way to associate pleasure with saving money. You can download FaceApp — which will give you a picture of what you will look like older and greyer, or you can take a deep breath just before spending money and ask yourself if you will regret the purchase later.

The easiest ways to waste money travelling are:

Getting a taxi. The solution to this is to always download the google map before you go. Many taxi drivers will drive you around for 15 minutes when the place you were trying to get to is a 5-minute walk… remember while not getting an overpriced taxi to tell yourself, 'I am saving money to free myself for more travel.'
Spending money on overpriced food when hungry. The solution: carry snacks. A banana and an apple will cost you, in most places less than a dollar.
Spending on entrance fees to top-rated attractions. If you really want to do it, spend the money happily. If you're conflicted sleep on it. I don't regret spending $200 on a skydive over the Great Barrier Reef, I do regret going to the top of the shard in London for $60. Only you can know but make sure it's your decision and not the marketing directors at said top-rated attraction.
Telling yourself 'you only have the chance to see/eat/experience it now'. While this might be true, make sure YOU WANT to spend the money. Money spent is money you can't invest, and often you can have the same experience for much less.

You can experience luxurious travel on a small budget which will trick your brain into thinking you're already a high-roller, which will mean you'll be more likely to start acting like one and invest your money. Stay in five-star hotels for $5 by booking on the day of your stay on booking.com to enjoy last minute deals. You can go to fancy restaurants using daily deal sites. Ask your airline about last minute upgrades to first-class or business. I paid $100 extra on a $179 ticket to Cuba from Germany to be bumped to Business Class. When you ask you will be surprised what you can get both at hotels and airlines.

Travel, as the saying goes is the only thing you spend money on that makes you richer. In practice, you can easily waste money, making it difficult to enjoy that metaphysical wealth. The biggest money saving secret is to turn bargain hunting into a pleasurable activity, not an annoyance. Budgeting consciously can be fun, don't feel disappointed because you don't spend the $60 to go into an attraction, feel good because soon that $60 will soon be earning money for you. Meaning, you'll have the time and money to enjoy more metaphysical wealth, while your bank balance increases.

So there it is, you can save a small fortune in The Maldives by being strategic with your trip planning. We've arranged everything in the guide to offer the best bang for your buck. Which means we took the view that if it's not a good investment for your money, we wouldn't include it. Why would a guide called 'Super Cheap The Maldives' include lots of overpriced attractions? That said if you think we've missed something or have unanswered questions ping me an email philgtang@gmail.com .I'm on central Europe time and usually reply within 8 hours of getting your mail.

Don't put your dreams off!

Time is a currency you never get back and travel is its greatest return on investment. Plus now you know you can visit The Maldives for a fraction of the price most would have you believe. Go to The Maldives and create unforgettable memories - on the cheap!

Thank you for reading

Dear Lovely Reader,

If you have found this book useful, please consider writing a short review on Amazon.

One person from every 1000 readers leaves a review on Amazon. It would mean more than you could ever know if you were one of our 1 in 1000 people to take the time to write a short review.

We are a group of four friends who all met travelling 15 years ago. We believe that great experiences don't need to blow your budget, just your mind.

Thank you so much for reading again and for spending your time and investing your trips future in Super Cheap Insider Guides.

One last note, please don't listen to anyone who says 'Oh no, you can't visit The Maldives on a budget'. Unlike you they didn't have this book. The truth is you can do ANY-WHERE on a budget with the right insider advice and planning. Sure, learning to travel to The Maldives on a budget that doesn't compromise on anything or drastically compromise on safety or comfort levels is a skill, but this guide has done the detective work for you. Now it is time for you to put the advice into action.

Phil

P.S If you need any more super cheap tips we'd love to hear from you e-mail me at philgtang@gmail.com, we have a lot of contacts in every region, so if there's a specific bargain you're hunting we can help you find it :-)

Dreaming of another tropical vacation? Check out our <u>Super Cheap Bora Bora guide</u>:

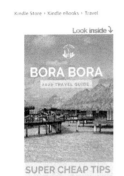

Look inside ↓

Super Cheap Bora Bora Travel Guide 2020: Enjoy a $5,000 trip to Bora Bora for under $1,900 (Budget Travel) Kindle Edition

by Phil G Tang (Author), William McBride (Author)

☆☆☆☆☆ ˅   4 ratings

⚡ Best Deal

› See all 2 formats and editions

Kindle	Paperback
$9.90	$12.99
Read with Our **Free App**	1 New from $12.99

Get this guide to tick Bora Bora off your bucket list for under $1,900 including flights.

Lonely Planet advises 'budget' travellers to pay $755 PER DAY to visit Bora Bora. This guide will show you how to comfortably enjoy two weeks in paradise for less than $1,900 or $135

Follow the Author

Websites to save you Money

1. **TalkTalkbnb.com** - Here you stay for free when you teach the host your native language
2. Rome2Rio.com - the go to site for good travel prices on train, bus, planes etc. Especially good for paths less travelled.
3. couchsurfing.com - stay for free with a local - always check reviews.
4. trustedhousesitter.com - always check reviews
5. booking.com - now sends you vouchers for discounts in the city when you book through them
6. airbnb.com for both accommodation and experiences.
7. https://trevallog.com/male-walking-tour/ - a self-guided Male walking tour.

SHOP 150 VACATIONS UNDER $150.

INCLUDING LONDON.

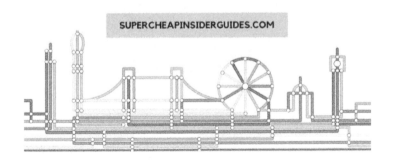

SUPERCHEAPINSIDERGUIDES.COM

Bonus Budget Travel Hacks

I've included these bonus travel hacks to help you plan and enjoy your trip to The Maldives cheaply, joyfully and smoothly. Perhaps they will even inspire you or renew your passion for long-term travel.

From saving space in your pack to scoring cheap flights, there are a wealth of generic travel hacks to help you enjoy stress-free, happier travels without breaking the bank. This is why I've included this bonus section to maximise the value you get from buying this book.

When I tell people I write a travel guide series focused on luxurious budget travel, they wrongly assume that's impossible and often say 'Hitchhiking and couch-surfing?'. Others with more vivid imaginations ask me if I recommend hooking up with older men or women... Of course, they are surprised when I tell them that not one of the 150 Super Cheap Guides endorses such practises because they maximise discomfort. They look at me dumbfounded and ask 'How on earth do you travel comfortably on a budget then?'

Travelling cheaply in a way that doesn't compromise enjoyment, comfort or safety is a skill I have honed over 20 years of travelling. My foremost learning was that locals always know the tricks and tips to enjoy the same or a better tourist experience for a 10th of the cost, and that's why I teamed up with locals in each locale to distil the tips that will save you a fortune without compromising on enjoyment or comfort.

Enjoyable budget travel is about balancing and prioritising what is important to you.
When I tell people about my methodology I often receive long defensive monologues about why they spend so much on travel, or why they can't or don't travel. Thats why we will first discuss how you can find the freedom to travel.

How to find the freedom to travel

Freedom is one of those words that can mean different things to different people. It's important to be clear on what it looks like to you in your life, and all the stories and beliefs that prevent you from having it. For me, freedom means always having at choice in my life. I don't do anything that I don't want to do. —LEO BABAUTA

We've spoken a lot about how to save money travelling to XXX, but how do you find the freedom if you have:

1. Pets
2. Kids
3. A spouse who doesn't want you to travel
4. A job that keeps you at home?

Like everything, there's a solution to every problem. In this chapter, I want to you to think about whether your excuses can be overcome using the following solutions, because as Randy Komisar said: "And then there is the most dangerous risk of all – the risk of spending your life not doing what you want on the bet you can buy yourself the freedom to do it later."

Pets

I have a dog, an extremely loving German Shepherd. And when I travel overland from Austria she comes with me and my wife. If we are heading on a longer trip we either leave her with friends or family or we get someone to house sit for us. housesitters.-com offers up people who are vetted and reviewed and in exchange for free accommodation will care for your pets. Just be aware it often works out financially better to rent your space on Airbnb and pay someone to look after your pets. Make sure you visit their facilities before you entrust your pet to anyone and of course, always read the reviews.

I know a lot of people miss their pets travelling which is why we endeavour to take our dog with us. Exploring with her has formed some of our most precious memories. If you're flying with your pet always look up the rules and make sure you comply. If you're going to the UK for example, they quarantine dogs who come in by air. So we only take our dog by car. Coming into the UK by car, dogs must need to be chipped, have a note from a vet saying they are clear of Rabies and tapeworms, have a pet passport and be on a course of medication for tapeworms 2 days before they enter. The UK is the strictest country I've encountered when it comes to travelling with pets so I use this as barometer. My point is, do your homework if you're bringing your furry friend, both about entry conditions and the local environment for your pet. For instance, in India, many domesticated dogs are attacked by street dogs. Educate yourself on your options and limitations but don't think because you have pets that travel is out of the question.

Kids

I also have a daughter who is about to turn 1. We have travelled to seven countries with her so far, with many more in the pipeline. The easiest way to travel with kids is in an RV. You don't have to worry about checking vast amounts of baggage or travelling with a stroller. You have unlimited freedom and can camp for free in many places. You can normally take the RV on a slow ship cheaper than the price of a plane ticket for 3 people.

A study by Cornell University found that we get more happiness from anticipating a travel experience in comparison to anticipating buying a new possession, so in that way, money can buy you happiness. If you invest in an RV, you can also turn it into a profit centre by renting it out on platforms like www.outdoorsy.com.

You don't necessarily have to fly to travel with kids, train, bus and RV's are better options. Kids become more adaptable and flexible when the world is their classroom. This is true at any age. but when kids immerse themselves in new places and engage with local cultures; this open-mindedness helps them in all aspects of their lives. For school-age children, you are limited to holiday dates, but with 12 weeks off a year, you can still find adventure together.

A spouse who doesn't want you to travel

A loving partner should always want what's best for you. Scientifically, travelling is proven to reduce stress. A study in 2000 study found that men and women who do not take a trip for several years are 30 per cent more likely to have a heart attack. It makes sense because when you travel you are more active; travellers often walk ten miles a day, sightseeing and soaking up new sights and smells.

Travelling also strengthens the 'openness' aspect of your personality and makes you less emotionally reactive to day-to-day changes, improving emotional stability. Sure, losing your baggage or almost missing a connecting flight can be panic-inducing, but, overall, the data supports that travelling is beneficial for you. Tell your partner about these studies, if they don't want a healthier, happier, more emotionally stable you, then it may be time to consider why you're investing your time with this person.

Another common issue is mismatched travel budgets. If you and your partner travel together and they force you to overspend with the 'we're on holiday/vacation!' appendage, here's a tip from one of our writers Kim:

'My husband and I were always having 'discussions' about money during our trips. I love bargains and he is the kind of traveller who's totally cool to be ripped off because he normally travels for business and has become used to spending corporate money. The compromise we reached is that he reads a shoestring or super cheap guide before the trip. Then when he wants to waste money, I say yes, but only in exchange for doing one budget item from the guide. It has worked wonders, lessened our 'discussions' and he now actually chooses cheaper destinations as he sees budgeting as a game.'

A job that keeps you at home

Our lives can feel constantly busy. Sometimes we may feel we are sinking beneath our workload. If you're close to or suffering a burnout the stress relief that comes from novelty and change in the form of new people, sights and experiences is the best remedy you could give to yourself.

If you're in a job that is hurting your health or well-being its time to reconsider why. It is often the case that you believe the work to be deeply rewarding, but if that reward leaves you ill, uninspired and fatigued, you can't help anyone. I learnt this the hard way when I worked for a charity whose mission I deeply resonated with. After 3 years of 70 hour work weeks, I'd lost hair, teeth, direction and, if I'm honest, faith in humanity. It took me 3 years to come back to the light and see that I chose a very stressful job that my body told me repeatedly it could not handle. Travel was a big part of forgiving myself. It helped me put old stories that held me back and probably sent me into this quagmire of self-abuse via work into perspective.

Sometimes we keep letting ourselves make excuses about why we're not travelling because we're scared of the unknown. In such cases, one of three things happens that forces a person from their nest:

- A traumatic event
- Completing a major milestone
- A sudden realisation or epiphany

Do yourself a favour, don't wait for any of those. Decide you want to travel, and book a flight. Our next section takes you through how to book the cheapest possible flight.

HOW TO FIND CHEAP FLIGHTS

"The use of travelling is to regulate imagination by reality, and instead of thinking how things may be, to see them as they are." S amuel Jackson

If you're working full-time you can save yourself a lot of money

by requesting your time off from work starting in the middle of the week. Tuesdays and Wednesdays are the cheapest days to fly, you can save hundreds just by adjusting your time off.

The simplest secret to booking cheap flights is open parameters. Let's say you want to fly from Chicago to Paris. You

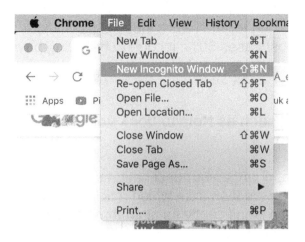

need to enter USA to France, you may find flights from NYC to Paris for $70 and can take a cheap flight to NYC. Make sure you calculate full costs, including if you need airport accommodation and of course getting to and from airports, but in every instance open parameters will save you at least half the cost of the flight.

If you're not sure about where you want to go, use open parameters to show you the cheapest destinations from your city.
Use skyscanner.net - they include the low-cost airlines that others like Kayak leave out.

Open parameters can also show you the cheapest dates to fly. If you're flexible you can save up to 80% of the flight cost. Always check the weather at your destination before you book, sometimes a $400 flight will be $20, because its monsoon season. But hey, if you like the rain, why not?

ALWAYS USE A PRIVATE BROWSER TO BOOK FLIGHTS

Skyscanner and other sites track your IP address and put prices up and down based on what they determine your strength of conviction to buy. e.g if you've booked one-way and are looking for the return these sites will jack the prices up by in most cases 50%. Incognito browsing pays.

Use a VPN such as Hola to book your flight from your destination

Install Hola, change your destination to the country you are flying to. The location from which a ticket is booked can affect the price significantly as algorithms take into account local buying power.

Choose the right time to buy your ticket.

Choose the right time to buy your ticket, as purchasing tickets on a Sunday has been proven to be cheaper. If you can only book during the week, try to do it on a Tuesday.

Mistake fares

Email alerts from individual carriers are where you can find the best 'mistake fares". This is where a computer error has resulted in an airline offering the wrong fare. In my experience its best to sign up to individual carriers email lists but if you ARE lazy Secret Flying puts together a daily roster of mistake fares. Visit   to see if there's any errors that can benefit you.

Fly late for cheaper prices.

Red-eye flights, the ones that leave later in the day, are typically cheaper and less crowded, so aim to book that flight if possible. You will also get through the airport much quicker at the end of the day, just make sure there's ground transport available for when you land. You don't want to save $50 on the airfare and spend it on a taxi to your accommodation.

Use this APP for same day flights

If you're plans are flexible, use 'Get The Flight Out' (
) a fare tracker Hopper that shows you
same-day deeply discounted flights. This is best for long-haul flights with major carriers. You can often find a British Airways round-trip from JFK Airport to Heathrow for $300. If you booked this in advance you'd pay at least double.

Take an empty water bottle with you

Airport prices on food and drinks are sky-high. It disgusts me to see some airports charging $10 for a bottle of water. ALWAYS take an empty water bottle with you. It's relatively unknown, but most airports have drinking water fountains past the security check. Just type in your airport name to
to locate the fountain. Then once
you've passed security (because they don't allow you to take 100ml or more of liquids) you can freely refill your bottle with water.

Round-the-World (RTW) Tickets

It is always cheaper to book your flights using a DIY approach. First, you may decide you want to stay longer in one country, and a RTW will charge you a hefty fee for changing your flight. Secondly, it all depends on where and when you travel and as we have discussed, there are many ways to ensure you pay way less than $1,500 for a year of flights. If you're travelling long-haul, the best strategy is to buy a return ticket, say New York to Bangkok and then take cheap flights or transport around Asia and even to Australia and beyond.

Frequent Flyer Memberships

A frequent-flyer program (FFP) is a loyalty program offered by an airline. They are designed to encourage airline customers to fly more to accumulate points (also called miles, kilometres, or segments) which can be redeemed for air travel or other rewards.

You can sign up with any FFP program for free. There are three major airline alliances in the world: Oneworld, SkyTeam and Star Alliance. I am with One World https://www.oneworld.com/members because the points can be accrued and used for most flights.

The best return on your points is to use them for international business or first class flights with lie-flat seats. You would need 3 times more miles compared to an economy flight, but if you paid cash, you'd pay 5 - 10 times more than the cost of the economy flight, so it really pays to use your points only for upgrades. The worst value for your miles is to buy an economy seat or worse, a gift from the airlines gift-shop.

Sign up for a family/household account to pool miles together. If you share a common address you can claim the miles with most airlines. You can use AwardWallet to keep track of your miles. Remember that they only last for 2 years, so use them before they expire.

Pack like a Pro

"He who would travel happily must travel light." – Antoine de St. Exupery 59.

Travel as lightly as you can. We always need less than we think. You will be very grateful that you have a light pack when changing trains, travelling through the airport, catching a bus, walking to your accommodation, or climbing stairs.

Make a list of what you will wear for 7 days and take only those clothes. You can easily wash your things while you're travelling if you stay in an Airbnb with a washing machine or visit a local laundrette. Roll your clothes for maximum space usage and fewer wrinkles. If you feel really nervous about travelling with such few things make sure you have a dressier outfit, a little black dress for women is always valuable, a shirt for men. Then pack shorts, long pair of pants, loose tops and a hoodie to snuggle in. Remind yourself that a lack of clothing options is an opportunity to find bargain new outfits in thrift stores. You can either sell these on eBay after you've worn them or post them home to yourself. You'll feel less stressed, as you don't have to look after or feel weighed down by excess baggage. Here are three things to remember when packing:

- Co-ordinate colours - make sure everything you bring can be worn together.
- Be happy to do laundry - fresh clothes when you're travelling feels very luxurious.
- Take liquid minis no bigger than 60ml. Liquid is heavy and you simply don't need to carry so much at one time.

Checks to Avoid Fees

Always have 6 months validity on your passport

To enter most countries you need 6 months from the day you land. Factor in different time zones around the world if your passport is on the edge. Airport security will stop you from boarding your flight at the airport if your passport has 5 months and 29 days left.

Google Your Flight Number before you leave for the airport

Easily find out where your plane is from anywhere. Confirm the status of your flight before you leave for the airport with flightaware.com. This can save you long unnecessary wait times.

Check-in online

The founder, Ryan O'Leary of budget airline RyanAir famously said: "We think they should pay €60 for [failing to check-in on-line] being so stupid.". Always check-in online, even for international flights. Cheaper international carriers like Scoot will charge you at the airport to check-in.

Checking Bags

Never, ever check a bag if you possibly can avoid it. It is always cheaper to put heavier items on a ship, rather than take them on a flight with you. Find the best prices for shipping at https://www.parcelmonkey.com/delivery-services/shipping-heavy-items

Use a fragile sticker

Put a 'Fragile' sticker on anything you check to ensure that it's handled better as it goes through security. It'll also be one of the first bags released after the flight, getting you out of the airport quicker.

If you do check your bag, photograph it

Take a photo of your bag before you check it. This will speed up the paperwork if it is damaged or lost.

Relaxing at the airport

The best way to relax at the airport is in a lounge where they provide free food, drinks, comfortable chairs, luxurious amenities (many have showers) and if you're lucky a peaceful ambience. If you're there for a longer time look for Airport Cubicles, sleep pods which charge by the hour.

You can use your FFP Card (Frequent Flyer Memberships) to get into select lounges for free. Check your eligibility before you pay.

If you're travelling a lot I'd recommend to Invest in a Priority Pass for the airport.
It includes 850-plus airport lounges around the world. The cost is $99 for the year and $27 per lounge visit or you can pay $399 for the year all inclusive.

If you need a lounge pass for a one-off day, you can get a Day Pass. Buy it online for a discount, it always works out cheaper than buying at the airport. Use   .

Lounges are also great if you're travelling with kids, as they're normally free for kids and will definitely cost you less than snacks for your little ones. The rule is that kids should be seen and not heard, so consider this before taking an overly excited child who wants to run around, or you might be asked to leave even after you've paid.

Money: How to make it, spend it and save it while travelling

How to earn money WHILE travelling

"Twenty years from now you will be more disappointed by the things you didn't do than by the ones you did do. So throw off the bowlines. Sail away from the safe harbour." - H. Jackson Brown

Digital nomads receive a lot of hype. Put simply they are "professionals who work online and therefore don't need to tie themselves to one particular office, city, or even country."

The first step in becoming a digital nomad, earning money while travelling is knowing what you can offer. Your market is the whole world. So, what product or service would you like to offer that they would pay for? Take some time to think about this. In German, they say you should do whatever comes easily to your hand. For example, I've always loved finding bargains, it comes very easily for me. Yet I studied Law and Finance at University, which definitely did not come easy. It's no shock that it didn't transpire into a career. And served more as a lesson in not following my ego.

There are thousands of possibilities to generate income while travelling; offering services like tutorial, coaching, writing service pr blogging. Most travellers I meet try their hand at blogging and earning from the advertisements. This is great if you have some savings, but if you need to earn straight away to travel, this should be on the back burner, as it takes time to establish. Still if this comes easily to you, do it!

You want to make good money fast. Ask yourself, what is it that you are good at and how can you deliver maximum value to other people? Here are some ideas if you're totally dumfounded:

1. Teaching English online - you will need a private room for this. Be aware that if you're from the USA and the country you want to work in requires a federal-level background check, it

may take months, so apply early. Opportunities are on: t.vip-kid.com.cn, abc360.com, italki.com, verbalplanet.com and verbling.com. You can expect to earn $20 an hour.

2. Work in a hostel. Normally you'll get some cash and free accommodation.
3. Fruit picking. I picked Bananas in Tully Australia for $20 an hour. The jobs are menial but can be quite meditative. Look on WWOOF.org for organic farm work.
4. fiverr.com - offer a small service, like making a video template and changing the content for each buyer.
5. Do freelance work online: marketing, finance, writing, App creation, graphic designer, UX or UI designer, SEO optimizer / expert. Create a profile on upwork.com - you need to put in a lot of work to make this successful, but if you have a unique skill like coding, or marketing it can be very lucrative.
6. Make a udemy.com course. Can you offer a course in something people will pay for? e.g. stock trading, knitting or marketing.
7. Use skype to deliver all manner of services: language lessons, therapy, coaching etc. Google for what you could offer. Most specialisms have a platform you can use to find clients and they will take a cut of your earnings/ require a fee.
8. You could work on luxury yachts in the med. Its hard work, but you can save money - DesperateSailors.com
9. Become an Airbnb experience host - but this requires you to know one place and stay there for a time. And you will need a work visa for that country.
10. Work on a cruise ship. This isn't a digital nomad job but it will help you travel and save at the same time.
11. Rent your place out on airbnb while you travel and get a cleaner to manage it. The easiest solution if you own or have a long-term rent contract.

How to spend money

Budget travel hacking begins with a strategy to spend without fees. Your individual strategy depends greatly on the country you legally reside in as to what cards are available. Happily there are some fin-tech solutions which can save you thousands and are widely available globally. I will address those first:

N26

N26 is a 10-year old digital bank. I have been using them for over 6 years. The key advantage is fee-free card transactions abroad. They have a very elegant app, where you can check your timeline for all transactions listed in realtime or manage your in-app security anywhere. The card you receive is a Mastercard so you can use it everywhere. If you lose the card, you don't have to call anyone, just open the app and swipe 'lock card'. It puts your purchases into a graph automatically so you can see what you spend on. You can open an account from abroad entirely online, all you need is your passport and a camera

Revolut

Revolut is a multi-currency account that allows you to hold and exchange 29 currencies and spend fee-free abroad. It's a UK based neobank, but accepts customers from all over the world.

TransferWise debit card

If you're going to be in one place for a long time the The TransferWise debit card is like having your travel money on a card – it lets you spend money at the real exchange rate.

Monzo

Monzo is good if your UK based. They offer a fee-free UK account. Fee-free international money transfers and fee-free spending abroad.

The downside

The cards above are debit cards, meaning you need to have money in those accounts to spend it. This comes with one big downside: safety. Credit card issuers' have "zero liability" mean-

ing you're not liable for unauthorised charges. All of the cards listed above do provide cover for unauthorised charges but times vary greatly in how quickly you'd get your money back if it were stolen.

The best option is to check in your country to see which credit cards are the best for travelling and set up monthly payments to repay the whole amount so you don't pay unnecessary interest. In the USA, Schwab[1] regularly ranks at the top for travel credit cards. Credit cards are always the safer option when abroad simply because you get your money back faster if its stolen and if you're renting cars, most will give you free insurance when you book the car rental using the card, saving you money.

---

[1] Charles Schwab High Yield Checking accounts refund every single ATM fee worldwide, require no minimum balance and have no monthly fee.

Always withdraw money; never exchange.

Money exchanges whether they be on the streets or in the airports will NEVER give you a good exchange rate. Do not bring bundles of cash. Instead withdraw local currency from the ATM as needed and try to use only free ATM's. Many in airports charge you a fee to withdraw cash. Look for bigger ATM's attached to banks to avoid this.

Recap:

- Take cash from local, non-charging ATMs for the best rates.
- Never change at airport exchange desks unless you absolutely have to, then just change just enough to be able get to a bank ATM.
- Bring a spare credit card for emergencies.
- Split cash in various places on your person (pockets, shoes) and in your luggage. Its never sensible to keep your cash or cards all in one place.
- In higher risk areas, use a money belt under your clothes or put $50 in your shoe or bra.

How to save money while travelling

Saving money while travelling sounds like an oxymoron, but it can be done with little to no effort. Einstein is credited as saying, "Compound interest is the eighth wonder of the world." If you saved and invested $100 today, in 20 years it would be $2,000 thanks to the power of compound interest. It makes sense then to save your money, invest and make even more money.

The Acorns app is a simple system for this. It rounds up your credit card purchases and puts the rest into a savings account. So if you pay for a coffee and its $3.01, you'll save 0.99 cents. You won't even notice you're saving by using this app:

Here are some more generic ways you can always save money while travelling:

Device Safety
Having your phone, iPad or laptop stolen is one BIG and annoying way you can lose money traveling. The simple solution is to use apps to track your devices. Some OSes have this feature built-in. Prey will try your smartphones or laptops (preyproject.com).

Book New Airbnb's
When you take a risk on a new Airbnb listing, you save money. Just make sure the hosts profile is at least 3 years old and has reviews.

If you end up in an overcrowded city

The website   is like Airbnb for
camping in people's garden and is a great way to save
money if you end up in a city during a big event.

Look out for free classes
Lots of hostels offer free classes for guests. If you're planning to stay in a hostel, check out what classes your hostel
offers. I have learnt languages, cooking techniques, dance
styles, drawing and all manner of things for free by taking
advantage of free classes at hostels.

Get a student discount card
If you're studying buy an ISIC card - International Student
Identity Card. It is internationally recognised, valid
in 133 countries and offers more than 150,000 discounts!

Instal
Maps me is extremely good for travelling without data. It's
like offline google maps without the huge download size.

Always buy travel insurance
Don't travel without travel insurance. It is a small cost to pay
compared with what could be a huge medical bill.

Travel Apps That'll Make Budget Travel Easier

Travel apps are useful for booking and managing travel logistics. They have one fatal downside, they can track you in the app and keep prices up. If you face this, access the site from an incognito browser tab.

Here are the best apps and what they can do for you:

- Best For flight Fare-Watching: Hopper.
- Best for booking flights: Skyscanner
- Best for timing airport arrivals: FlightAware - check on delays, cancellations and gate changes.
- Best for overcoming a fear of flying: SkyGuru - turbulence forecasts for the route you're flying.
- Best for sharing your location: TripWhistle - text or send your GPS coordinates or location easily.
- Best for splitting expenses among co-travellers: Splittr, Trip Splitter, Venmo or Splitwise.

We have covered the best apps and websites for XXX in the section above called useful websites.

How NOT to be ripped off

"One of the great things about travel is that you find out how ma
ny good, kind people there are."
— Edith Wharton

The quote above may seem ill placed in a chapter entitled how
not to be ripped off, but I included it to remind you that the vast
majority of people do not want to rip you off. In fact, scammers
are normally limited to three situations:

1. Around heavily visited attractions - these places are targeted
   purposively due to sheer footfall. Many criminals believe rip-
   ping people off is simply a numbers game.
2. In cities or countries with low-salaries or communist ideolo-
   gies. If they can't make money in the country, they seek to
   scam foreigners. If you have travelled to India, Morocco or
   Cuba you will have observed this phenomenon.
3. When you are stuck and the person helping you knows you
   have limited options.

Scammers know that most people will avoid confrontation.
Don't feel bad about utterly ignoring someone and saying
no. Here are six strategies to avoid being ripped off:

**1. Never ever agree to pay as much as you want. Always
    decide on a price before.**
Whoever you're dealing with is trained to tell you, they are unin-
terested in money. This is a trap. If you let people do this they will
ask for MUCH MORE money at the end, and because you have
used there service, you will feel obliged to pay. This is a con-
man's trick and nothing more.

2. Pack light
You can move faster and easier. If you take heavy luggage you
will end up taking taxi's which are comparatively very costly over
time.

3. NEVER use the airport taxi service. Plan to use public transport before you reach the airport.

4. Don't buy a sim card from the airport. Buy from the local supermarkets it will cost 50% less.

5. Eat at local restaurants serving regional food
Food defines culture. Exploring all delights available to the palate doesn't need to cost huge sums.

6. Ask the locals what something should cost, and try not to pay over that.

7. If you find yourself with limited options. e.g. your taxi dumps you on the side of the road because you refuse to pay more (common in India and parts of South America) don't act desperate and negotiate as if you have other options or you will be extorted.

8. Don't blindly rely on social media

Let's say you post in a Facebook group that you want tips for travelling to The Maldives. A lot of the comments you will receive come from guides, hosts and restaurants doing their own promotion. It's estimated that 50% or more of Facebook's current monthly active users are fake[2]. And what's worse, a recent study found Social media platforms leave 95% of reported fake accounts up[3]. These accounts are the digital versions of the men who hang around the Grand Palace in Bangkok telling tourists its closed, to divert you to

---

2

3

shops where they will receive a commission for bringing you.

It can also be the case that genuine comments come from people who have totally different interests, beliefs and yes, budgets to yours. Make your experience your own and don't believe every comment you read.

Bottom line: use caution when accepting recommendations on social <u>media</u> and always fact-check with your own research.

Small tweaks on the road add up to big differences in your bank balance

Take advantage of other hotel's amenities

If you fancy a swim but you're nowhere near the ocean, try the nearest hotel with a pool. As long as you buy a drink, the hotel staff will likely grant you access.

Fill up your mini bar for free.

Fill up your mini bar for free by storing things from the breakfast bar or grocery shop in your mini bar to give you a greater selection of drinks and food without the hefty price tag.

Save yourself some ironing

Use the steam from the shower to get rid of wrinkles in clothing. If something is creased, leave it trapped with the steam in the bathroom overnight for even better results.

See somewhere else for free

Opt for long stopovers, allowing you to experience another city without spending much money.

Wear your heaviest clothes

on the plane to save weight in your pack, allowing you to bring more with you. Big coats can then be used as pillows to make your flight more comfortable.

Don't get lost while you're away.

Find where you want to go using Google Maps, then type 'OK Maps' into the search bar to store this information for offline viewing.

Use car renting services

Share Now or Car2Go allow you to hire a car for 2 hours for $25 in a lot of Europe.

Share Rides

Use sites like blablacar.com to find others who are driving in your direction. It can be 80% cheaper than normal transport. Just check the drivers reviews.

Use free gym passes

Get a free gym day pass by googling the name of a local gym and free day pass.

When asked by people providing you a service where you are from..

If there's no price list for the service you are asking for, when asked where you are from, Say you are from a lesser-known poorer country. I normally say Macedonia, and if they don't know where it is, add it's a poor country. If you say UK, USA, the majority of Europe bar the well-known poorer countries taxi drivers, tour operators etc will match the price to what they think you pay at home.

Set-up a New Uber/ other car hailing app account for discounts

By googling you can find offers with $50 free for new users in most cities for Uber/ Lyft/ Bolt and alike. Just set up a new gmail.com email account to take advantage.

Where and How to Make Friends

"People don't take trips, trips take people." – John Steinbeck

Become popular at the airport

Want to become popular at the airport? Pack a power bar with multiple outlets and just see how many friends you can make. It's amazing how many people forget their chargers, or who packed them in the luggage that they checked in.

Stay in Hostels

First of all, Hostels don't have to be shared dorms, and they cater to a much wider demographic than is assumed. Hostels are a better environment for meeting people than hotels, and more importantly they tended to open up excursion opportunities that further opened up that opportunity.

Or take up a hobby

If hostels are a definite no-no for you; find an interest. Take up a hobby where you will meet people. I've dived for years and the nature of diving is you're always paired up with a dive buddy. I met a lot of interesting people that way.

When unpleasantries come your way...

We all have our good and bad days travelling, and on a bad day you can feel like just taking a flight home. Here are some ways to overcome common travel problems:

Anxiety when flying

It has been over 40 years since a plane has been brought down by turbulence. Repeat that number to yourself: 40 years! Planes are built to withstand lighting strikes, extreme storms and ultimately can adjust course to get out of their way. Landing and take off are when the most accidents happen, but you have statistically three times the chance of winning a huge jackpot lottery, then you do of dying in a plane crash.

If you feel afraid on the flight focus on your breathing saying the word 'smooth' over and over until the flight is smooth. Always check the airline safety record on airlinerating.com I was surprised to learn Ryanair and Easyjet as much less safe than Wizz Air according to those ratings because they sell similarly priced flights. If there is extreme turbulence, I feel much better knowing I'm in a 7 star safety plane.

Wanting to sleep instead of seeing new places

This is a common problem. Just relax, there's little point doing fun things when you feel tired. Factor in jet-lag to your travel plans. When you're rested and alert you'll enjoy your new temporary home much more. Many people hate the first week of a long-trip because of jet-lag and often blame this on their first destination, but its rarely true. Ask travellers who 'hate' a particular place and you will see, that very often they either had jet-lag or an unpleasant journey there.

Going over budget

Come back from a trip to a monster credit card bill? Hopefully this guide has prevented you from returning to an unwanted bill. Of course, there are costs that can creep up and this is a reminder about how to prevent them making their way on to your credit card bill:

- To and from the airport. Solution: leave adequate time and take the cheapest method - book before.
- Baggage. Solution: take hand luggage and post things you might need to yourself.
- Eating out. Solution: go to cheap eats places and suggest those to friends.
- Parking. Solution: use apps to find free parking
- Tipping. Solution Leave a modest tip and tell the server you will write them a nice review.
- Souvenirs. Solution: fridge magnets only.
- Giving to the poor. (This one still gets me, but if you're giving away $10 a day - it adds up) Solution: volunteer your time instead and recognise that in tourist destinations many beggars are run by organised crime gangs.

Price v Comfort

I love traveling, I don't love struggling. I like decent accommodation, being able to eat properly and see places and enjoy. I am never in the mood for low cost airlines or crappy transfers so here's what I do to save money.

- Avoid organised tours unless you are going to a place where safety is a real issue. They are expensive and constrain your wanderlust to typical things. I only recommend them in Algeria, Iran and Papua New Guinea - where language and gender views pose serious problems all cured by a reputable tour organiser.
- Eat what the locals do.
- Cook in your airbnb/ hostel where restaurants are expensive.
- Shop at local markets.
- Spend time choosing your flight, and check the operator on arilineratings.com
- Mix up hostels and Airbnbs. Hostels for meeting people, Airbnb for relaxing and feeling 'at home'.

Not knowing where free toilets are

Use Toilet Finder - https://play.google.com/store/apps/details?id=com.bto.toilet&hl=en

Your airbnb is awful

Airbnb customer service is notoriously bad. Help yourself out. Try to sort things out with the host, but if you can't, take photos of everything e.g bed, bathroom, mess, doors, contact them within 24 hours. Tell them you had to leave and pay for new accommodation. Ask politely for a full refund including booking fees. With photographic evidence and your new accommodation receipt, they can't refuse.

The airline loses your bag

Go to the Luggage desk before leaving the airport and report the bag missing.
Most airlines will give you an overnight bag, ask where your staying and return the bag to you within three days. Its extremely rare for them to completely lose it due to technological innovation, but if that happens you should submit an insurance claim after the

three days is up, including receipts for everything your had to buy in the interim.

Your travel companion lets you down.

Whether it's a breakup or a friend cancelling, it sucks and can ramp up costs. The easiest solution to finding a new travel companion is to go to a well-reviewed hostel and find someone you want to travel with. You should spend at least three days getting to know this person before you suggest travelling together. Finding someone in person is always better than finding someone online, because you can get a better idea of whether you will have a smooth journey together. Travel can make or break friendships.

Culture shock

I had one of the strongest culture shocks while spending 6 months in Japan. It was overwhelming how much I had to prepare when I went outside of the door (googling words and sentences what to use, where to go, which station and train line to use, what is this food called in Japanese and how does its look etc.). I was so tired constantly but in the end I just let go and went with my extremely bad Japanese. If you feel culture shocked its because your brain is referencing your surroundings to what you know. Stop comparing, have Google translate downloaded and relax.

Your Car rental insurance is crazy expensive

I always use carrentals.com and book with a credit card. Most credit cards will give you free insurance for the car, so you don't need to pay the extra.

You're sick

First off ALWAYS, purchase travel insurance. Including emergency transport up to $500k even to back home, which is usually less than $10 additional. I use https://www.comparethemarket.com/travel-insurance/ to find the best days. If I am sick I normally check into a hotel with room service and ride it out.

Make a Medication Travel Kit

Take travel sized medications with you:

- Antidiarrheal medication (for example, bismuth subsalicylate, loperamide)
- Medicine for pain or fever (such as acetaminophen, aspirin, or ibuprofen)
- Throat Lozenges

Save yourself from most travel related hassles

- Do not make jokes with immigration and customs staff. A misunderstanding can lead to HUGE fines.

- Book the most direct flight you can find, nonstop if possible.

- Carry a US$50 bill for emergency cash. I have entered a country and all ATM and credit card systems were down. US$ can be exchanged nearly anywhere in the world and is useful in extreme situations, but where possible don't exchange, as you will lose money.

- Check, and recheck, required visas and such BEFORE the day of your trip. Some countries, for instance, require a ticket out of the country in order to enter. Others, like the

US and Australia, require electronic authorisation in advance.

- Airport security is asinine and inconsistent around the world. Keep this in mind when connecting flights. Always leave at least 2 hours for international connections or international to domestic. In London Stansted for example, they force you to buy one of their plastic bags, and remove your liquids from your own plastic bag.... just to make money from you. And this adds to the time it will take to get through security so lines are long.

- Wiki travel is perfect to use for a lay of the land.

- Expensive luggage rarely lasts longer than cheap luggage, in my experience. Fancy leather bags are toast with air travel.
-

Food

- When it comes to food, eat in local restaurants, not tourist-geared joints. Any place with the menu in three or more languages is going to be overpriced.
- Take a spork - a knife, spoon and fork all in one.

Water Bottle

Take a water bottle with a filter. We love these ones from Water to Go.
Empty it before airport security and separate the bottle and filter as some airport people will try and claim it has liquids…

Bug Sprays

If you're heading somewhere tropical spray your clothes with Permethrin before you travel. It lasts 40 washes and saves space in your bag. A 'Bite Away' zapper can be used after the bite to totally erase it. It cuts down on the itching and erases the bite from your skin.

Order free mini's

Don't buy those expensive travel sized toiletries, order travel sized freebies online. This gives you the opportunity to try brands you've never used before, and who knows, you might even find your new favourite soap.

Take a waterproof bag

If you're travelling alone you can swim without worrying about your phone, wallet and passport laying on the beach. You can also use it as a source of entertainment on those ultra budget flights.

Make a private entertainment centre anywhere

Always take an eye-mask, earplugs, a scarf and a kindle reader - so you can sleep and entertain yourself anywhere!

The best Travel Gadgets

The door alarm

If you're nervous and staying in private rooms or airbnbs take a door alarm. For those times when you just don't feel safe, it can help you fall asleep. You can get tiny ones for less than $10 from Amazon:

Smart Blanket

Amazon sells a 6 in 1 heating blanket that is very useful for cold plane or bus trips. Its great if you have poor circulation as it becomes a detachable Foot Warmer: Amazon http://amzn.to/2hTYlOP I paid $49.00.

The coat that becomes a tent

https://www.adiff.com/products/tent-jacket. This is great if you're going to be doing a lot of camping.

Clever Tank Top with Secret Pockets

Keep your valuables safe in this top. Perfect for all climates.

on Amazon for $39.90

Optical Camera Lens for Smartphones and Tablets
Leave your bulky camera at home. Turn your device into a high-performance camera. Buy on Amazon for $9.95

Travel-sized Wireless Router with USB Media Storage

Convert any wired network to a wireless network. Buy on Amazon for $17.99

Buy a Scrubba Bag to wash your clothes on the go
Or a cheaper imitable. You can wash your clothes on the go.

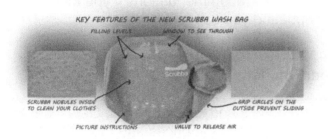

Hacks for Families

Rent an Airbnb apartment so you can cook

Apartments are much better for families, as you have all the amenities you'd have at home. They are normally cheaper per person too. We are the first travel guide publisher to include Airbnb's in our recommendations if you think any of these need updating you can email me at philgtang@gmail.com

Shop at local markets

Eat seasonal products and local products. Get closer to the local market and observe the prices and the offer. What you can find more easily, will be the cheapest

Take Free Tours

Download free podcast tours of the destination you are visiting. The podcast will tell you where to start, where to go, and what to look for. Often you can find multiple podcast tours of the same place. Listen to all of them if you like, each one will tell you a little something new.

Pack Extra Ear Phones

If you go on a museum tour, they often have audio guides. Instead of having to rent one for each person, take some extra earphones. Most audio tour devices have a place to plug in a second set.

Buy Souvenirs Ahead of Time

If you are buying souvenirs, something touristy, you are paying a premium price. By ordering the exact same product online from sites like Aliexpress.com, you save a lot of money and hassle. You can have them shipped to your home address so you don't have to carry them around, but still have something to give friends and family when you return.

Use Cheap Transportation

Do as the locals do, including checking out weekly passes.

Carry Reusable Water Bottles

Spending money on water and other beverages can quickly add up. Instead of paying for drinks, take some refillable water bottles.

Combine Attractions

Many major cities offer ticket bundles where one price gets you into 5 or 6 popular attractions. You will need to plan ahead of time to decide what things you plan to do on vacation and see if they are selling these activities together.

Pack Snacks

Granola bars, apples, baby carrots, bananas, cheese crackers, juice boxes, pretzels, fruit snacks, apple sauce, grapes, and veggie chips.

Stick to Carry-On Bags

Do not pay to check a large bag. Even a small child can pull a carry-on.

Visit free art galleries and museums

Just google the name + free days.

Eat Street Food

There's a lot of unnecessary fear around this. You can watch the food prepared. Go for the stands that have a steady queue.

Travel Gadgets for Families

Dropcam

Are what-if scenarios playing out in your head? Then you need Dropcam.

'Dropcam HD Internet Wi-Fi Video Monitoring Cameras help you watch what you love from anywhere. In less than a minute, you'll have it setup and securely streaming video to you over your home Wi-Fi. Watch what you love while away with Dropcam HD.'

Approximate Price: $139

Kelty-Child-Carrier

Voted as one of the best hiking essentials if you're traveling with kids and can carry a child up to 18kg.

Jetkids Bedbox

No more giving up your own personal space on the plane with this suitcase that becomes a bed.

Safety

"If you think adventure is dangerous, try routine. It's lethal." –
Paulo Coelho

Backpacker murdered is a media headline that leads people to think traveling is more dangerous than it is. The media sensationalise the rare murders and deaths of backpackers and travellers. The actual chances of you dying abroad are extremely extremely low.

Let's take the USA as an example. In 2018, 724 Americans **died** from unnatural causes, 167 died from car accidents, while the majority of the other deaths resulted from drownings, suicides, and non-vehicular accidents. Contrast this with the 15,000 murders in the US in 2018, and travelling abroad looks much safer than staying at home.

There are many thing you can to keep yourself save. Here are out tips.

1. Always check fco.co.uk before travelling. NEVER RELY on websites or books. Things are changing constantly and the FCO's (UK's foreign office) advice is always UP TO DATE (hourly) and extremely conservative.
2. Check your mindset. I've travelled alone to over 180 countries and the main thing I learnt is if you walk around scared, or anticipating you're going to be pickpocketed, your constant fear will attract bad energy. Murders or attacks on travellers are the mainstay of media, not reality, especially in countries familiar with travellers. The only place I had cause to genuinely fear for my life was Papa New Guinea - where nothing actually happened to me only my own panic over culture shock.

There are many things you can do to stop yourself being victim to the two main problems when travelling: theft or being scammed.

I will address theft first. Here are my top tips:

- Stay alert while you're out and always have an exit strategy.
- Keep your money in a few different places on your person and your passport somewhere it can't be grabbed.
- Take a photo of your passport on your phone incase. If you do lose it, google for your embassy, you can usually get a temporary pretty fast.
- Google safety tips for traveling in your country to help yourself out and memorise the emergency number.
- At hostels keep your large bag in the room far under the bed/ out of the way with a lock on the zipper.
- On buses/trains I would even lock my bag to the luggage rack.
- Get a personal keychain alarm. The sound will scare anyone away.
- Don't wear any jewellery. A man attempted to rob a friend of her engagement ring in Bogota, Colombia, and in hindsight I wished I'd told her to leave it at home/wear it on a hidden necklace, as the chaos it created was avoidable.
- Don't turn your back to traffic while you use your phone.
- When traveling in the tuktuk sit in the middle and keep your bag secure. Wear sunglasses as dust can easily get in your eyes.
- Don't let anyone give you flowers, bracelets, or any type of trinket, even if they insist it's for free and compliment you like crazy.
- Don't let strangers know that you are alone - unless they are travel friends ;-)
- Lastly, and most importantly -Trust your gut! If it doesn't feel right, it isn't.

Hilarious Travel Stories

I have compiled these short stories from fellow travellers to pick you up when you're feeling down. Life on the road isn't always easy and we've all had those days when we want to stay in bed and forget the world exists. Laughter is the best way I know to shake those feelings. All people who have shared these stories wanted to remain anonymous. After reading them I think you'll understand why...

I mentioned my wife earlier, so its only fair she be the first story. Don't worry she has given me permission to share.

A marriage up the wall

'Delhi belly got me on the third day into the trip to India. I was vomiting so much that I couldn't keep even water down so I went to a health clinic for tourists. Whilst I was there I was asked to poop into a jar and happily put on a drip.

The doctor attending me was mid to late 40's and very creepy. I decided I'd leave the clinic after my 4th bag of fluids because I felt better and was weirded out by the intense stares of my doctor. As I was paying the bill, the doctor came over, dropped to one knee and asked me to marry him at the desk. I stuttered in shock that I was already was married. He was holding a jar of my poo in his hand, stood and then chucked it at the wall. The jar broke open and my watery specimen was literally smeared across the wall as he trudged off. The woman serving me bobbed her head from side to side as if we were discussing the weather and said 'its not personal madam, you look like his last wife.'

Glass shame

'I was in Nashville airport in the smoking room. I heard my name being called for my flight so I rushed out but instead of rushing through the door, I walked smack into the glass. When I opened the door the entire departure lounge was roaring with laughter.'

The Dashing Date

'I had a date with a fellow Brit in Medellin. I went to the bathroom and when I came back, I asked him if he had paid the bill and he replied 'yes'. We were going down some stairs when he suddenly shouted at me to run. Yes, the restaurant staff were running after us because he hadn't paid.'

A fear of farting in hostels

'When I arrived to stay in my first ever hostel in London, I realised I had an intense fear
farting in my sleep. I literally gave myself such bad constipation I had to go to hospital. It turns out an enema is worse than hostel farting.'

What a boob

I fell on the Tube in London getting into a carriage. Unfortunately I managed to grab a woman's boob on the way to the floor. I was so mortified I walked everywhere else during the trip.'

Cementing a few laughs

'I was walking on the streets in Singapore when they were fixing the roads. I somehow stepped in fresh cement. I only noticed when my feet became so heavy I thought I had twisted my ankle. The cement got so hard, I had to take my shoes off as I couldn't pick up my feet. Locals were very clearly entertained as I walked back to my accommodation in my sponge bob squarepants socks.

If you've got a hilarious travel story you'd love to share, email me at   . All identifying details will be removed.

How I got hooked on budget travelling

'We're on holiday' is what my dad used to say to justify getting us in so much debt we lost our home and all our things when I was 11. We moved from the suburban bliss of Hemel Hempstead to a run down council estate in inner-city London, near my dad's new job as a refuge collector, a fancy word for dustbin man. I lost all my school friends while watching my dad go through a nervous breakdown.

My dad loved walking up a hotel lobby desk without a care in the world. So much so, that he booked overpriced holidays on credit cards. A lot of holidays. As it turned out we couldn't afford any of them. In the end, my dad had no choice but to declare bankruptcy. When my mum realised he'd racked up so much debt our family unit dissolved. A neat and perhaps as painless a summary of events that lead me to my life's passion: budget travel that doesn't compromise on fun, safety or comfort.

I started travelling full-time at the age of 18. I wrote the first Super Cheap Insider guide for friends visiting Norway - which I did for a month on less than $250. When sales reached 10,000 I decided to form the Super Cheap Insider Guides company. As I know from first-hand experience debt can be a noose around our necks, and saying 'oh come on, we're on vacation' isn't a get out of jail free card.

Before I embarked upon writing Super Cheap Insider guides many, many people told me that my dream was impossible, travelling on a budget could never be comfortable. I hope this guide has proved to you what I have known for a long-time: budget travel can feel luxurious when you know and use the insider hacks.

And apologies, if I depressed you with my tale of woe. My dad is now happily remarried and works as a chef in London at a fancy hotel - the kind he used to take us to!

A final word...

There's a simple system you can use to think about budget travel. In life we can choose two of the following: cheap, fast or quality. So if you want it Cheap and fast you will get a lower quality service. Fast-food is the perfect example. The system holds true for purchasing anything while travelling. I always choose cheap and quality, except in times where I am really limited on time. Normally you can make small tweaks to make this work for you. Ultimately you must make choices about what's most important to you.

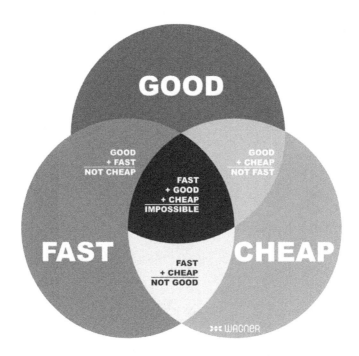

Our Writers

Phil Tang was born in London to immigrants, Phil graduated from The London School of Economics with a degree in Law. Now he travels full-time in search of travel bargains with his wife, dog and 1 year old daughter.

Ali Blythe has been writing about amazing places for 17 years. He loves travel and especially tiny budgets equalling big adventures nearly as much as his family. He recently trekked the Satopanth Glacier trekking through those ways from where no one else would trek. Ali is an adventurer by nature and bargainist by religion.

Michele Whitter writes about languages and travel. What separates her from other travel writers is her will to explain complex topics in a no-nonsense, straightforward way. She doesn't promise the world. But always delivers step-by-step methods you can immediately implement to travel on a budget.

Kim Mortimer, Kim's input on Super Cheap Insider Guides show you how to stretch your money further so you can travel cheaper, smarter, and with more wanderlust. She loves going over land on horses and helps us refine each guide to keep them effective.

Congratulations, you've saved money and done Good!

We donate 10% of all book profits to charity.

This year we are donating to Animal Shelters. Dogs are illegal on The Maldives. I have never seen a dog in the Maldives, let alone a stray. Dogs are considered unclean by muslims. They are prohibited and even in the immigration form received on the plane to the capital Male is clear that dogs are forbidden. Only cats are found on the island, and other local animals.

'My dog Gracie was abandoned on the highway in Slovakia. At just ten months old, they tied her to the railings and left her there. Animal Hope picked her up and took care of her and found her a home with us. She is now a healthy, happy girl and loves travelling with us, getting her nose into new smells and soliciting belly rubs from fellow travellers. What breaks my heart is her 'I haven't been abandoned dance'. She is always so happy that we haven't abandoned her when we collect her from outside a supermarket that she dances on her leash for several minutes. Watch her 'I haven't been abandoned dance' dance   . Money could never buy the happiness she has brought my family and me, but donations can help other abandoned animals like her to find loving homes.'

Katherine Huber, a contributor to Super Cheap Vienna.

Donations are made on the 4th January of each year on profits from the previous year. To nominate a charity to receive 10% of the proceeds of sales from our 2021 editions complete the form here: supercheapinsiderguides.com

Gracie

Copyright

HOW DID WE DO?

1 DID WE SAVE YOU MONEY?

2 DID YOU LEARN INSIDER INSIGHTS?

3 DID YOU GET A LIST OF THE BEST CHEAP EATS?

4 DID WE HELP YOU PLAN TO SAVE AND ENJOY MORE?

WHAT CAN WE DO BETTER?

EMAIL ME: PHILGTANG@GMAIL.COM

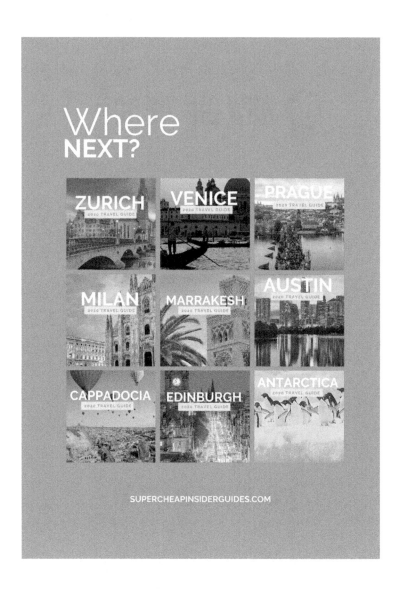

Made in the USA
Las Vegas, NV
08 January 2022